DIRK WILLEMS

Dirk Willems was a Dutch Anabaptist who, in the late winter of 1569 was identified and, under the laws of Holland, the thief catcher of Asperen came to arrest him for his faith. Running for his life, Dirk came to an ice covered lake. After making his way across in great peril, he realised his pursuer had fallen through into the freezing water. Turning back, Dirk ran to the struggling man and dragged him safely to the shore. He was then arrested. The thief catcher wanted to release Dirk, but the burgomaster, who had appeared on the scene, insisted that Dirk be bound, taken off to prison, interrogated and tortured in an unsuccessful effort to make him renounce his faith. He was tried and found guilty of having been re-baptised, of holding secret meetings in his home, and of allowing baptism there. All of these things he confessed to freely. For his act of great goodness he received in return imprisonment, torture and death. Here is an embodiment of some of the great strengths of the Anabaptists.

A BELIEVING CHURCH

KEITH G JONES

A BELIEVING CHURCH

Learning From Some Contemporary Anabaptist and Baptist Perspectives

KEITH G JONES

Easter 1998

The Baptist Union of Great Britain

British Library Cataloguing in Publication Data.

A catalogue record for this book is available from the British Library.

ISBN 1-898077-38-X

Published by the Baptist Union of Great Britain
Baptist House, PO Box 44, 129 Broadway, Didcot, Oxfordshire,
OX11 8RT

Printed in Great Britain by GEM Publishing Company,
Brightwell, Wallingford, Oxfordshire

DEDICATION

To Alex and Tim,

may they be inheritors of a Christocentric, baptistic and radical church

CONTENTS

Acknowledgments   xi

Foreword   xiii

I   Introduction   1

II   A Believing Church   9

III   Who were the Anabaptists?   15

IV   Anabaptist issues   33

V   Where to now?   53

VI   The Schleitheim Confession: The Seven Articles   57

VII   Glossary of Terms   63

VIII   Bibliography   67

ACKNOWLEDGMENTS

Thanks are due to the following for permission to use copyright material:-

Judson Press, (Valley Forge, Pa, USA) for the woodcut of Balthasar Hubmaier, from *Balthasar Hubmaier: Anabaptist Theologian and Martyr* by Torsten Bergsten, edited by W R Estep, Jr. Copyright © 1978

Herald Press, (Scottdale, PA 15683, USA) for the illustrations of Dirk Willems (cover) and the two young ladies executed in the bishopric of Bamberg, from *Martyrs Mirror* by Thieleman J van Braght.

Herald Press, (Scottdale, PA 15683, USA) for the *Seven Articles of the Schleitheim Confession*, from *The Legacy of Michael Sattler* translated and edited by John H Yoder. © 1973 All rights reserved.

FOREWORD

Post-modernism: we hear a lot these days about an era without a "master narrative", without certainties shared throughout society. Post-Christendom: increasingly we are realizing that in our world Christians can no longer assume that their views will dominate the public agenda. This new world has been on the way for a long time, but recent events have made us acutely aware of them. How can we bear witness to the Christian good news in post-modernity and post-Christendom?

As a Baptist minister and leader, Keith Jones constantly thinks about these questions. He knows that for many the response to a loss of control and certainty is despair, or a desperate search for some quick solution to perplexing problems. But he is also a theologian and a historian. As a theologian, he knows that throughout the Bible God in crisis situations showed his people the way forward by reminding them of God's actions in the past. So the "origin stories" of the past - the Exodus, the Law, the life, death and resurrection of Jesus Christ, Pentecost - can be a means of healing the present, and of restoring hope and direction to God's people. As a historian, Keith believes that this is also true of church history. For Baptists, about whose life and witness he cares passionately, history can be not simply dull facts that probationers need to memorize; history can be a means that God uses to renew the church.

This is where the Anabaptists enter. Keith Jones, in this potent and pertinent book, believes that the Radicals of the Reformation have relevance for Baptists in the post-Christian, post-Christendom world of the end of the second millennium. This relevance is partly because their story is powerful; he rightly points to people like Dirk Willems or Maeyken Boosers whose remarkable actions raise questions about our priorities and fears. But this relevance is also because their witness is corporate and demonstrable; he believes that this is the way that today's church will have a future.

Keith Jones knows that from the early 17th century onwards English Baptists have differed in their views of their continental Anabaptist cousins. Scholars have debated what influence the Dutch Mennonites had on the origins of the Baptist movement in this country; and church leaders have fluctuated in their attitudes to the Anabaptists. These debates, as Keith recognizes, will go on. But his contribution is this: he believes that "ideas have wings", and that the ideas of the Reformation Radicals are walking into our time in a way that can transform the life and witness of Baptist churches in three ways.

First, the Anabaptist way that Keith Jones introduces us to is a way of discipleship centred in Jesus Christ. In an era of competing truth claims, the Christian church needs to point to Jesus as the one whose person, work and teaching fundamentally query contemporary values and hold out the offer of something better. Jesus, radiating the forgiving love of the Father, joyfully deviant, shining truth into the darkest places of his age, is good news in our age, too. Wealth, war, worry, power - these Sermon on the Mount issues are perennial. The Anabaptist way, in a way that other traditions have not always been, is Christocentric.

Second, Keith demonstrates that the Anabaptist way is corporate. His phrase "the gathering church" points to his understanding; for us Christians there is salvation when we are gathered together into the Body of Christ. So baptism means dying to individualism, and rising into the corporate life of the people of God. It means dying to exclusive, hierarchical, patriarchal patterns of church life, and rising to the communal life of people who are learning how to share their lives, their wealth, their meal tables, in Christ. In a post-modern world of personal dislocation and isolation, the Anabaptist way is communitarian.

Third, the corporate way must always be practical. He shows how the Anabaptist way has insisted that truth must be more than words - it must make a demonstrable difference in the way that Christians live. Truth is not only thought and "believed"; in order to be persuasive, it is lived and embodied. So the Anabaptists, listening to Jesus and the New Testament church, have addressed issues of peacemaking, truthfulness, and the sharing of wealth and power. These things change people and transform their communities of faith. In our world words are cheap and arguments are easily dismissed as representing this or that power interest, but there is no argument so strong as a community of people whose life together is a manifestation of a truth - of a reality - that is deeper than argument. The Anabaptist way posits that the key to the witness of a missionary congregation will be demonstration.

Throughout this book, Keith Jones helpfully highlights his own passions and concerns. His wide experience in talking with Christians of non-baptistic traditions is reflected in his discussion of Anabaptist ecumenism; other characteristic themes are his concern for human rights, and for congregations who find Christ in their midst as they gather together at the Table. His knowledgeable love of the centuries of English Baptist history is also apparent. He is clearly rooted in Baptist traditions. And yet he calls for an assessing of tradition in light of the "origin stories" of Jesus and of early Anabaptist and Baptist history. The significance of the past for the future isn't always clear. Yet throughout his work he helpfully raises questions for discussion and debate. This book contains not roadmaps but signposts for the future.

Keith Jones' book is the product of his own commitment to follow Jesus and to encourage a church whose witness is vital. In a post-modern, post-Christendom world, I commend it to you. It can stimulate our thinking and point us all to a life of faith that is Christocentric, corporate and practical.

Alan Kreider
Oxford
14 February 1998

I INTRODUCTION

In the contemporary ferment of Christian life in a post-Christian, so-called post-modern Europe, there is a serious challenge to all Christian believers as to what sort of church is appropriate and what sort of mission will enable effective engagement with people. On the one hand our calling is to be faithful to the Gospel as we have come to understand it, whilst on the other we are challenged to be effective missionary communities in the society and culture in which we are set.

This is not a new challenge. The church, from the first generation and down through the centuries, has sought to understand and be true to the good news in Jesus, whilst approaching society with an appropriate mission strategy.

Being true to our past

In every generation the people of God have struggled with the desire to feel in continuity with the first communities of faith - knowing what is of the essence of the church of Jesus Christ - and the attempt to be authentic and relevant to the communities in which they are set. The interaction between the two is a constant dynamic. The story of the people of God has thus been one where reform, renewal, reformation and reaction have been in creative tension. Indeed, if we were not a people concerned with reformation and renewal we might well be seen as those who had closed ourselves off to the influence and work of the Holy Spirit. Some of the attempts at renewal have led into by-ways, heresy, failure. That is almost inevitable. There are moments when reaction may provide wise checks and balances in the search for authentic faith. At other times there have been developments of profound significance out of which new bursts of missionary energy, the renewal of spiritual life and the deepening of the understanding of being the people of God have come.

Reform and renewal

Some reform and renewal have been born out of a recovery of insights from the past. On other occasions the Holy Spirit has opened up new truths within the truth which we know in Jesus. Some reforms have been classified, almost universally, as a "good thing", to use the words of *1066 and all that*. Some other events have received a bad press. On the whole the various individuals and diverse communities classified as "Anabaptist" have, for many people, been known by the 'bad press'. The violent events in 1534 at Münster, in north west Germany, with the attempt to establish a radical theocracy and the subsequent suppression by the Roman Catholic forces, have been seen as an unfortunate moment in the history of the church.

The radicals of the pre-Reformation and Reformation era, "Anabaptists" are sometimes much more interesting and diverse than that one group in Münster. From their insights have grown some of the great Christian world communions. A mark of many has not been the sword, associated with Münster, but the peace-church tradition.

The purpose

This modest booklet attempts to uncover some key themes from the Radical Reformation period and ask the question, "what might these themes mean for us today as we, in our own time and circumstance, seek to be part of the way the Holy Spirit is renewing the church?"

It is written specifically into the general Christian perspective of the Free Churches and with a particular English Baptist slant. At the outset there is an on-going debate about the links between the Radical Reformation, the Anabaptists and the major Anglo-Saxon and north American traditions which belong in the Independent, Baptist and Congregational traditions. That point will be explored later. There is no attempt to say that this is one neat, logical, genetic family. However, as we look at history from the time of John Wyclif to Dan Taylor (two fellow Yorkshiremen) we are struck again and again by the recurrence of certain themes and the interaction of certain players.

I am aware of the dangers of writing a specialist booklet which might, to quote the distinguished historian, A J P Taylor, be "100% right, but 90% useless." This booklet aims to take up some key themes from an Anabaptist and Baptist perspective and try, in a non-technical way, to raise issues which might be relevant to us and our quest to be God's missionary people today.

Ideas have wings

We live in the days of the Internet and e-mail, where an idea, or even a joke, told in one part of the world is, within seconds, commonplace in another part of the world by means of electronic media. We assume today that ideas have wings. No, more than that, ideas move faster than the speed of light! It may have been slower in the fourteenth and fifteenth centuries, but we must realise that even before the advent of printing there was much traffic amongst scholars in Europe. With the advent of printing, the Magisterial Reformers - Luther, Zwingli and Calvin, together with their followers, were soon engaged in the exchange of ideas and debate across Europe in a way which fuelled the outbreak of reform and renewal at an outstanding pace.

From Oxford to Prague

Take as an example the practice which had grown up in the medieval church of denying the cup at the Eucharist to lay people. John Wyclif (c1329-1384), the early English radical and pre-reformer, had been concerned in his writings about ecclesiology, or doctrine of the church, and the nature of the Eucharist, or Lord's Supper. These ideas were read with great interest by Jan Hus and his friends in Prague, and in 1414 Jacob Mies of the historic Charles University in Prague, formally defended in debate the then novel idea that lay people should receive both bread and wine at the Eucharist. By 1433 in the Prague Compacts, the Roman Catholic hierarchy, all the way to the Vatican, conceded that the laypeople in Bohemia could receive the Eucharist in both kinds. Subsequently, it was regarded as a key Hussite (the followers of Jan Hus) doctrine and a

Reformation principle, but the birth of the idea came from Wyclif. The practice was expounded and defended publicly in the Catholic church, and receiving both bread and wine in the Eucharist was allowed before the key period of the Reformation. Though the action was subsequently rescinded by the Pope in the aftermath of the major events of the Reformation in the early 1500s, the fact is that the issue was discussed and the insights of Wyclif travelled half way round Europe. Ideas have wings!

Networking in Paris

John Calvin studied at the Royal College in Paris where one of his teachers was John Major from Scotland, a disciple of Duns Scotus, who had taught at Oxford from 1297-1301. John Major was also an exponent of the theory of knowledge and logic included in the nominalism of William of Occam. In this school Calvin learnt how to doubt the metaphysical powers of reason. This, so Kilian McDonnell believes, is why Calvin the reformer had so little time for speculation. Indeed the Sorbonne in Paris and the university in Oxford had many contacts. Calvin was subject to many of the great intellectual ideas being debated across Europe in a pre-reformation debate. Ideas have wings - medieval Scotland to Oxford, to Paris, to Geneva, then back to Scotland.

Connections

These two examples, relating to the same general period of the history of the church, though not to the heart of the Anabaptist vision, are meant simply to make the point that there was much contact between scholars and reformers. There is no need to have instant access to the Internet to appreciate that in the story of the people of God, Christian communities have been stimulated in reform and renewal, reaction and response, together, not in isolation. A concern rediscovered or amplified in one place, may, through exchange of writings, academic discourse, the journeying of Christian travellers, be taken, worked with, and reformulated in another place, where it may have an even greater impact on the life of the believers.

Therefore we might reasonably suppose that the 'family' of the Radical Reformation stimulated one another. Ideas recurred amongst the children and cousins of the Radical Reformation - Hussites, Hutterites, Mennonites, Amish, Baptists, Congregationalists, Quakers, Levellers, Diggers and the like. Yes, there were differences of emphasis. There developed a stream of evangelical Anabaptists in whom, perhaps, we are more interested. Some groups became less orthodox in Christian belief. Other groups brought fresh insights and in due course there would be counter-reaction.

A believers' church

Within this 'family' many issues were worked at. Certain themes were common to all. Some themes, for instance, peace and peacemaking, occur in only parts of this loose family. Other concerns about the church as a gathered community of believers subject to no civil authority are more general. Some suffered from a degradation because of their extreme application. Others were never fully explored.

Re-examining the Anabaptist vision

Today, in many parts of the world there is a desire to re-examine the radical Anabaptist vision and to ask what lessons we might learn for the contemporary church and our mission. This re-working of the past starts, for our time, in the work of the US Mennonite, Harold S Bender and his *Anabaptist Vision* (1943). In the British Isles much is owed to the Baptist World Alliance and Mennonite contacts involving people like the late Ernest A Payne.

The Anabaptist circle

More recently the work of Alan and Ellie Kreider, Mennonite Missionaries to the UK, has been very significant in a European context. The development of the Institute for Baptist and Anabaptist studies at the International Baptist Theological Seminary, now based in Prague, has raised interest amongst many Baptists in insights from the Anabaptists.

The growth in England in the 1990s of the Anabaptist Network, bringing together Mennonites, Baptists, Anglicans, new church leaders and others, has started a fresh round of discussion on the life, spirituality and theology of the early Anabaptists. In the mid 1990s the development of the Anabaptist Theological Study Circle, involving several key British scholars such as Christopher Rowland, Nigel Wright, Brian Haymes, Martin Scott, Ruth Gouldbourne, Stuart Murray and others has begun a key task in applying ecumenical scholarly reflection to these issues. I have been privileged to be a part of that group. Now Spurgeon's College offer a degree in Anabaptist and Baptist studies validated by the University of Wales.

A pilgrimage

We have come a long way from the anathema often associated in the popular mind with the Anabaptists because of Münster.

This booklet is simply a taster. It is not meant to be a scholarly study of the various Anabaptist communities - how they came into being, what their distinctives were, where they went to. A bibliography and resource section at the end is provided for those whose appetite is whetted. Rather, it is an attempt to open up for reflection, discussion and debate some of the key theological insights and church practices of the various Anabaptist groups which might present a challenge to our own pattern of Christian discipleship, or an insight into how we can more effectively be the church of Jesus Christ in our day and age.

My conviction is that the story of the various evangelical Anabaptist groups is a story related in some important ways to the first General Baptists. The ideas of these groups were part of the ferment of reflection and discourse which pervaded northern Europe, including the British Isles. In that sense the Particular Baptist tradition would not have been unaware of the issues raised and the reflection which developed. There is, of course, nothing so unique about that period of the history of the church which leads me to argue "if only we could return there all would be well". There are those who have believed it is right to go back, whether to the reformation era or the first century, and seek to recreate a "true church" based on exact following of their models. This is not the view I am advocating. There is no simple way back. The culture, society, the mission dynamic have all changed. However, I am persuaded that unless we look carefully at our history and learn from it, we might well miss something of a larger vision and the opportunity to reconnect with some of our roots. Here, I dare to believe, is one means of revisioning ourselves for the mission task in our generation. Be encouraged to look for the positive insights in your own situation.

Rediscovering the Radical Reformation

This booklet is an attempt to offer to local churches in the believers' church tradition some insights from the past which could well be a help as we face the contemporary missionary challenge. This is a very modest attempt to help people engage in serious reflection on how we open ourselves to being the faithful church of Jesus Christ today and what our mission commitment and strategy should be. It is not an essay in recovering historical information for its own sake. No, the only value in this exercise is to help us reflect together on how, under the guidance of the Holy Spirit, we can be the missionary people of God.

On dates and spellings

I have struggled to come to a clear mind about whether to include dates. In the case of key figures in the story I have given dates, where known, to provide some insight as to the time frame. Many Anabaptists met an early end - martyrs to the Radical Reformation, either at the hands of Catholic or Protestant rulers. There is much dispute and little accurate information about the date and place of birth of some key figures. In many instances I have given an approximate and commonly accepted date of birth. As a "new European" my inclination is always to use the accepted localised spelling of a town or city. However, on reflection I decided against turning Prague into Praha, Vienna into Wein and Zurich into Zürich.

With regard to the names of individuals I have tended to use Anglicised forms, though with the occasional idiosyncratic variation which indulges my own temperament and normal usage!

On the absence of footnotes

As I have stated earlier, this is not a scholarly work in the technical sense. It is a popular work to encourage you to think things through for yourself. Therefore, I have not provided any footnotes. However, at the end of the booklet I have provided a reading list for those who wish to explore original writings, those who want to read up on the history, who seek divergent views and those who want to keep pace with the contemporary debate.

A note of thanks

Wayne Pipkin first encouraged me to look deeper at the Anabaptists. Jim McClendon has provided in his systematic theology a baptistic approach which has greatly helped my own reflection. My thanks are due to them. I am grateful to Alan Kreider, Faith Bowers, Ruth Gouldbourne and John Briggs for reading early drafts of this manuscript. Their comments have stopped me making some errors. They have helped me immensely. However, they bear no responsibility for the inadequacies of the finished text. Hilary Bradshaw, Maureen White and my wife, Denise, have done much by way of sub-editing and turning the text into print-ready copy. My thanks, as always, are due to them.

Keith G Jones
McLean, Virginia
December 1997

II A BELIEVING CHURCH

The first English Baptists

Scholars and historians debate where English Baptists come from. The first Baptist church in modern times was formed in Holland in the seventeenth century by a group of dissenting religious exiles from the eastern counties of England. Leaders amongst that group were John Smyth and Thomas Helwys. They had fled from England to escape persecution by the state church and to be free to worship as a gathered company of disciples and in a way they believed God was leading them. There they came into contact with, and were helped by, the followers of an Anabaptist group which had been kept alive by the remarkable itinerant ministry of Menno Simmons. It must be remembered that the Anabaptist movement was, itself, fragmented and developed in different ways in various locations throughout Europe. Whilst there are some common themes, particularly related to ecclesiology, it is a naïve view to suggest that in every tenet of action and approach Anabaptist communities in Switzerland, south Germany, Bohemia, Holland and England shared every aspect of belief and church life in common.

Of course, these groups did not choose the name Anabaptist. It was given to them by others. It was at first a disparaging nickname. It was a term of abuse employed by many, but later it came to be a description bearing testimony to people of deep faith with a strong desire to be true to their Christian pilgrimage.

In Holland, Smyth and Helwys entered into discussion with Mennonite Anabaptists about the nature of baptism and whether it should be applied to infants as a sign of the covenant into which they entered, or whether baptism should be in accord with the model they perceived in the New Testament. This they saw as the action of the church on those who had heard the Gospel and responded in a faith commitment. They struggled greatly with this. What was involved? Who should baptize? Whether, as English separatists, they could baptize themselves, or whether baptism should be sought from those who previously had been baptized as believers?

For Smyth and Helwys and their followers this was a defining moment in the development of their separatist convictions into those of the gathered church practising the baptism of believers on their profession of faith. The debate with the followers of Menno Simmons led to different decisions. Smyth baptized himself and then his followers, but wondered whether this had been the right thing to do. Later he applied to join the Mennonite church. Helwys and his friends returned to England to bear testimony to what they had discovered in their reflection with the Mennonites. The first English Baptist church had been formed, albeit on Dutch soil, and from that movement some returned to England to begin what became the General Baptist churches. Others joined the Pilgrim Fathers in going to colonial north America and others continued with the Mennonites.

Anabaptists on English soil

However, it is a mistake to believe that that was the first occasion when Anabaptist ideas had flourished on English soil. With the Act of Supremacy in 1534 the English church was separated from Rome and the Church of England began to be shaped. Reform started to happen from within and as the debate progressed, insights from the continental Reformation were discussed and debated. England was perceived to be a place of religious tolerance and some escaping persecution elsewhere came to find refuge until the years of Queen Mary temporarily reversed the trend. Amongst those who made the journey were Anabaptists. They added to the ferment which had found its roots in John Wyclif and the Lollards, had been stirred by Luther and his theology, and was being influenced by the Swiss Reformation and Huldrych Zwingli, not to mention other actors on the stage of reform such as Andrew Karlstadt (c1477-1541). Still to come was the heady stuff of John Calvin. The presence of foreign Anabaptists in England was, as William Estep remarks, soon marked by martyrdom. Irvin B Horst suggests the number of Anabaptists burned by Henry VIII and Queen Mary was larger than the number of Lollards burned in the previous century. This fact may still surprise you, for a popular reading of English church history will tell you much about the Lollards, but little about the Anabaptists - almost the forgotten people of the Reformation.

This pattern of martyrdom continued throughout the reign of Mary, but even though a terrible war of attrition was waged against them the ideas and theological insights of Anabaptists became part of the Radical Reformation ferment in England. Estep suggests, for instance, that the Brownists and Barrowists gained insights which developed their ecclesiology. Indeed, I believe the comment of Estep, that the very concept of the gathered church, which is at the heart of the separatist tradition, was Anabaptist in origin and not a conscious product of the Magisterial Reform developments we associate with Luther, Zwingli and Calvin. None of those great reformers and their disciples clearly articulated an ecclesiology of the churches composed of committed disciples only.

The views of Baptist historians

Now, to take such a stand is in contradiction to some Baptist scholars and you must weigh the evidence for yourself. The earliest English Baptist historians, Crosby (1738) and Ivimey (1811) were concerned with the development of the movement against infant baptism and classed all such movements as Baptist. Evans (1862) sees the two movements as related. In 1905 J C Carlile felt the General Baptists, "besides being in substantial theological agreement with the Anabaptists adopted their form". This view is contested by W T Whitley (1923), H Wheeler Robinson (1937), A C Underwood (1945) and B R White (1971). E A Payne argued for the complexity of the relationships and for some ideas being clearly taken on board alongside some theological precepts of the Magisterial Reformers (Luther, Zwingli, Calvin and their successors). In this he is supported by Mervyn Himbury (1962), Albert W Wardin (1995), W R Estep (1986) and, to a lesser extent, H Leon McBeth (1987). W H Brackney in his 1988 book *The Baptists*, one in a series of American Denominational histories, says -

> *There will never be an answer (as to our origins) which satisfies all or even most Baptists since there is no date, no place, and no person to whom all can look with complete confidence, as the locus classicus of the movement.*

Ian Sellers (1981), reviewing the debate about Baptist origins, appears to suggest that when Baptists have wanted to emphasize their radicalism they claim an affinity with the Anabaptists, and when they have wanted to emphasize their respectability they have disavowed these connections. Dr Sellers suggests -

> *Perhaps in the end it is on the skilful choice of terminology that future research on Baptist/Anabaptist relationships will depend. Possibly we have reached a stage where the startling metaphor may shed more light than the learned treatise.*

Ideas have wings

My prime desire is to take forward the notion that, as Ernest Payne argued, ideas have wings. One key strand of English Baptist life developed clear links with the Anabaptist movement. The other strand, the Particular Baptists, were born out of a separatist tradition which had developed, in the ferment of reformation. Both developed an ecclesiology which some leading scholars declare owes part of its inspiration to the Radical Reformation associated with some important groups of Anabaptists.

In those circumstances the theologising, the developing of the notions and content of the gathered believers' church has a fresh relevance for those who belong to the expression of Christianity called Baptist. This finds a focus in the concept of God gathering people together in communities of committed discipleship; where to be drawn into that community demands a declared faith commitment; where those already gathered administer, on a profession of faith, the New Testament sacrament of Baptism; where the baptism of such a believer marks the identification and the incorporation of that person into a faith community engaged in communal discipleship and sharing a particular missionary ideology.

This "baptist" gathered community is distinct. Though some Baptists have borrowed, often very inadequately, aspects of the theology of the Magisterial Reformers, (a partial insight from Zwingli in terms of the Eucharist; some aspects of the systematic theology of John Calvin and so on), the motif of the baptist vision is rooted in the Anabaptist concept of God gathering the believers who profess faith in Christ in baptism and who are joined together in true fellowship, *koinonia*, as a group of committed disciples. From this, other things follow, but this is the starting point and the related aspects and consequences are a challenge to the contemporary Christian.

So, let us look at those early Anabaptists in all their variety and with all their enthusiasm so that we can appreciate the spread of this key element in the Radical Reformation movement.

III WHO WERE THE ANABAPTISTS?

The radical ecclesiological and missiological insights which marked out the Anabaptists can be traced in every generation of the story of the Christian church. Certainly Anabaptist insights and values did not start afresh with events in Europe in the fifteenth century. However, for the purpose of this exploration we are not going to look at the history of radical biblical Christians from the first assembly in the closed room in Jerusalem, through to our gathered churches today. Some of the themes featured have been part of the story of the Christian church in nearly every generation. Undoubtably, in the generations immediately preceding the sixteenth century Reformation in Europe, there were various preliminary events which should be looked at carefully by those interested in a detailed scholarly pursuit of these arguments.

Radical Reformers

So, we will not explore the story of my fellow Yorkshireman John Wyclif (c1330-1384) nor the details of the life and work of the Czech reformer Jan Hus, sometime Rector of the Charles University in Prague (c1372-1415) whom Wyclif greatly influenced, much less the stirrings created by Girrolamo Savonarola (1452-98), but it would be foolish to claim that radical reforming ideas began, without a pre-history, in Canton Zurich in the 1520s.

Renaissance and Christian Humanism

The climate for reformation in the western church had been developing for some time. The Renaissance had played its part in creating an intellectual environment where the status quo of the dominance of the

Pope and his officers, both in matters of state politics and in the life of the church, could not go unchallenged. The causes of the Renaissance were deep and broad. Norman Davies says -

> They can be related to the growth of cities and of late medieval trade, to the rise of rich and powerful capitalist patrons, to technical progress which affected both economic and artistic life. But the source of the spiritual developments must be sought above all in the spiritual sphere.

The Reformation, like the Renaissance, found root in the world of ideas. The church was in a malaise; corruption and lack of vision were the order of the day. There was a strong attitude of anticlericalism. Common people were irritated by the wealth of the church, angered at compulsory tithes, offended by clerical power and unchastity. Writers and thinkers set out to challenge the prevailing attitudes from within, like most reforming movements, but the biblical insight about new wine and old wineskins was never truer.

The Christian Humanists, as they were called, began to spring up in centres of learning throughout Europe. All might have echoed the comment of one of their lesser brethren, Cyriac of Ancona: 'I go to wake the dead.'

Erasmus of Rotterdam (c1466-1536)

The leading figure amongst them was Erasmus of Rotterdam. Gerhard Gerhards, a Dutchman, better known by his pen names 'Desiderius' and 'Erasmus', was the principal practitioner of Christian humanism. He travelled widely visiting, amongst other places, London, Cambridge and Basle. In the great universities of Europe his ideas were talked about, discussed and developed. His preface to his Greek New Testament (1516) read -

> I wish that every woman might read the Gospel and epistles of St. Paul. Would that these were translated into every language..... and understood not only by Scots and Irishmen but by Turks and Saracens. Would the farmer might sing snatches of scripture at his plough, that the weaver might hum phrases of Scripture to the tune of his shuttle.

Erasmus, though critical of the Church, did not go all the way in the search for reformation. In our contemporary world some criticise this Christian humanism for giving rise to the notion of the autonomous self. To others, it marked the beginning of the liberation of Europe from authoritarian and ultimately destructive influences.

Whilst the Renaissance was not the sole birth-source of the Reformation, it provided an intellectual climate which, matched with the spiritual experiences of certain key scholars, created the setting in which the Reformation could flourish. In that activity there were a whole host of thinkers and writers, theologians and priests, noblemen and peasants who became drawn into change, which occurred throughout northern Europe and took hold on a permanent basis in significant areas.

Three Magisterial Reformers

Three figures stand out as the Magisterial Reformers - Martin Luther (1483-1546), a Professor of Theology in Wittenburg; Huldrych Zwingli (1484-1531), a correspondent of Erasmus, who in 1519 became town preacher in Zurich in German speaking Switzerland; and Jean Calvin (1509-1564) a French scholar, who was persuaded in 1541 to oversee the reformation in Geneva.

Many Baptists assert that the roots of their own life and theology lie with the Calvinistic developments in Geneva and, whilst there is some truth in that assertion, it is far from being completely the case. Rather, it is with Huldrych Zwingli in Zurich and his friends and colleagues that the radical reformation and the Anabaptist theology and insights, which mark the 'Baptist' story, might be said to own their origin.

Huldrych Zwingli (c1484-1531)

Zwingli was appointed town preacher in the well fortified city of Zurich, a flourishing capital with an industrious population of 7,000 inhabitants. The government was in the hands of two burgomasters with small and large councils in support. There were seven churches in the city, and it was to the main church, the Great Minster, that Zwingli was appointed town preacher. Zurich was in the Diocese of Constance, but the Bishop had little influence in the city. It was the Council which exercised spiritual supervision over the lives of the citizens.

At the Frauminster, on the other side of the Limmat River, Wilhelm Reublin (c1482-1560) was the preacher from 1522 and he became involved in the general ferment and debate. He was the first priest to marry publicly in 1523, following a petition to the bishop by Zwingli, and was the first to preach against infant baptism. He was later banished from Zurich, but appeared in Waldshut to baptize Hubmaier in 1525. For a while he was pastor of the Anabaptist congregation in Wytikon, five miles south east of Zurich.

One of the aims of Zwingli was to promote increased reading of the Bible and he established what became known as the Prophezei school in the Great Minster, a cold, forbidding building which still stands by the Limmat river. Here the three languages of Latin, Greek and Hebrew were studied, so that the Scriptures could be read. Two of those involved were Conrad Grebel and Felix Mainz. The group gathered early in the morning in the choir stalls. Zwingli would open with prayer -

Almighty, eternal and most merciful God, whose word is a lantern to our feet and a light to our path, open and enlighten our hearts that we may understand your holy word in its purity and holiness and do those things that we have rightly understood so that we may in no way offend your majesty, through Jesus Christ Our Lord, Amen.

Then one of the students would read a passage from the Scriptures to be expounded. This was done in Latin. The Old Testament passage was read in Hebrew and expounded in Hebrew and Latin, following which the same passage would be read in Greek from the Septuagint, comparing translation and insight, scripture against scripture. Finally, a preacher set out in the local Swiss German tongue what had been gleaned in the earlier work, concluding in prayer.

Grebel (c1498-1526), Mainz (c1498-1527) and Blaurock (d1529) - the first Swiss Anabaptists

In this setting the Scriptures were opened up and after a time Grebel, Mainz, Blaurock and others became convinced that the true church, as formed in the New Testament and understood in the Scriptures, was a gathering of believers, not something imposed and controlled by the city authorities. Zwingli and his friends parted company on this point. He saw the need for the church-state link to preserve the reforming work going on and to validate the community. At first Zwingli began to question the validity of infant baptism on scriptural grounds, but recanted of that view, again seeing the problem of breaking a tie between being a citizen of Zurich from birth and being part of the church in Zurich.

The first Anabaptist congregation

The friends parted and by January 1525 a group of believers were meeting, talking and praying together in what might be regarded as the first church of the Anabaptist movement in the Reformation era. The first believers' baptism in Switzerland took place on 21 January 1525. Johann Kessler, chronicler of St Gallen, writing from the State Church perspective, recorded the event like this -

> *In this it became clear why they sought with such fervour and rigour to overthrow infant baptism: in order that if it was wiped out, it would be necessary if one wished to be a Christian at all to be baptized again, one and all; thereby their plan to separate would be achieved and their assemblies would gain a great increase. For this reason, they, the aforementioned arch-Anabaptists, Conrad Grebel first of all, baptized one another at home at night as true testimony that they considered infant baptism to be no baptism, but theirs was the true baptism, and likewise their assemblies (where the true baptism was) they considered to be the holy Christian Church.*

From that, the first Anabaptist church was formed at Zollikon, a village near Zurich. It was soon being persecuted, but the ideas of the group there found echoes amongst others who had been set free by the insights of

Christian humanism and the anticlericalist critique and reforming atmosphere breaking out throughout western and central Europe. It is worth noting that Felix Mainz became the first Protestant to die at the hands of Protestants in 1527. George Blaurock was burned at the stake in 1529.

Balthasar Hubmaier (c1480-1528)

Balthasar Hubmaier, a professor of theology at the University of Ingoldstadt, later residing in Waldshut, a town near to Zurich, but across the border in Germany, was a humanist who had read Luther and Melancthon and took a keen interest in the Reform movement in Zurich, participating in the regular disputations held there. By 1523 he was questioning infant baptism and in 1526 wrote against it. He was to become the most serious theologian of the early Anabaptist movement. His eighteen articles set out his own reforming position, which had many similarities to the views of Zwingli. However, his book, *On the Christian Baptism of Believers,* was a direct refutation of Zwingli and a stand for believers' baptism. Hubmaier and sixty others were baptized in Waldshut, Bavaria on Easter Day, 1525 by the Anabaptist ex-priest, Wilhelm Reublin from Canton Zurich.

Hubmaier was pursued by Catholic and Reformed enemies across south Germany and Moravia. In the course of his journeys he stayed in Augsburg where it is possible he met Hans Hut, the bookseller and disciple of Müntzer. In Moravia he spent time with the Czech Brethren, the Hussites (followers of the pre-reformer Jan Hus), or Unitas Fratarum, whom he regarded as sharing many of the same insights as the Anabaptists. The Catholic authorities captured him, accused him of being an arch-heretic possessed with devils and he was taken to Vienna. King Ferdinand of Bohemia ordered that he be burnt at the stake and this took place on 10 March 1528.

Balthasar Hubmaier

The only known portrait. From an old woodcut.

Michael Sattler (c1490-1527) and the Schleitheim Confession

The ferment in Canton Zurich had spread into southern Germany and beyond. A key moment came in the south German community of Schleitheim, on the Schaffhausen side of the Rhine. There Michael Sattler developed the Anabaptist movement and in 1527, in a major conference of Anabaptist leaders, he revealed his Confession, a statement of Anabaptist convictions on seven crucial issues, agreed just two years after the real emergence of the movement. This document, the Schleitheim Confession, has been a source of great interest to those seeking to understand and interpret the Anabaptist vision.

Michael Sattler had been a Prior at a Benedictine monastery in the Black Forest of southern Germany. He may still have been there when in 1525 this monastery was captured by a peasant war band during the widespread unrest which some historians call the Peasants' War and which began in Waldshut, Bavaria, the previous year. Waldshut, was, of course, the place where Hubmaier was developing his Anabaptist teachings, and peasants from there were part of the group who arrived at the monastery. Did Sattler meet and talk with them? We do not know, but by 1525 his Anabaptist convictions were sufficient for him to be at the heart of the Schleitheim debate. He believed in the necessity of being obedient to Scripture and argued against the more apocalyptic views of people such as Hans Hut. John Howard Yoder, the Mennonite scholar, regards Schleitheim as the "crystallization point" for Swiss Anabaptism. Harold Bender takes the view that Wilhelm Reublin was the person who influenced him most.

Sattler, from his monastic background, appears to have seen Anabaptism as producing a new rule for Christian living. In his short time as an Anabaptist before his arrest, trial and execution, he debated with other Anabaptists on key points within the emerging movement. Over against Hans Hut, an apocalyptic evangelist, he was concerned that the people of God should be seeking to be obedient to Christ, rather than concerned for the future.

With Balthasar Hubmaier he debated whether society could be reformed as a whole. Hubmaier, the humanist, urbane scholar was hopeful that it could be. Sattler, the ex-Prior held fast to the notion of two distinct "kingdoms" and the necessity for the gathered community of believers to separate from the world.

With the very spiritual Hans Denck he debated the place of Scripture. Early Anabaptists sought to explore the importance and relationship between the "Word" and the "Spirit" - a contemporary enough theme! Sattler held to the primacy of the Scriptures and the necessity of relying on these as the source of life, not allowing them to be generalised or spiritualised away.

Austria and South Germany

The developments from the Prophezei school and the debates which Zwingli held in Zurich, in the humanist reform climate, soon led to Anabaptist ideas spreading throughout southern Germany and Austria. Hubmaier took part in disputations, and as the trained theologian of the movement he became key to developments. Others soon joined him developing Anabaptist gathered congregations in various regions. Hans Denck, known by some as the "apostle of love", in a spiritual movement, sought to build bridges in what was rapidly becoming a divided age. His oft-quoted phrase "No one can truly follow Christ, except he follow him in life", might be seen as an authentic mark of the heart of the Anabaptist approach.

Pilgram Marpeck (c1490-1556)

Pilgram Marpeck was an author and leader amongst the south German Anabaptists from about 1530 to 1556. A native of the Tyrol, Austria, it is possible that Marpeck grew up in the Bavarian town of Rosenheim and moved to Rattenberg, Austria, where his father, Heinrich, served as a councillor, mayor and district magistrate. He received a "scholarly education", which can be discerned from his writings. He worked in mining as a purchasing agent and later a mining magistrate. In 1528 he was removed from office for refusing to assist in catching Anabaptists. It is presumed he adopted Anabaptist teachings in about 1525. From 1532 until 1544 he lived in Switzerland and moved around in the Tyrol, Moravia and southern Germany. He established congregations and had contact with Hutterites and Swiss Brethren. By 1544 he was in Augsburg leading an Anabaptist congregation. Four works have been attributed to Marpeck - *Clear Response; Clear and Useful Instruction; The Exposure of the Babylonian whore;* and *Confession.* Marpeck affirmed the divinity of Christ, but stressed Christ's historical, physical humanity. He believed that the Bible is properly understood only of and by the whole community of believers and perhaps, more clearly than any other early Anabaptist, presented a coherent theology of the primacy of the New Testament over the Old. Marpeck wrote the following meditation in which he described springtime in God's vineyard -

> *The vines have sprouted blossoms and exude fragrance, that is, the planting of the heavenly Father which He has planted are the true believers in Christ Jesus. Through the sap of grace from Christ the vine, they develop blossoms that they may see God's working in them through His plantings in Christ and give God praise, in Christ Jesus.*

Caspar Schwenckfeld in Strassbourg

In 1529 a Silesian nobleman, Caspar Schwenckfeld, arrived in Strassbourg as a reformer and a refugee from Catholic and Lutheran disputes. He was a courtier who had first been attracted to the ideas of Martin Luther, but later became concerned at what he saw as the over-emphasis on justification by faith. Schwenckfeld longed also to see the reform of the life of the individual. Strassbourg at that time was a melting pot of the Reformation. Martin Bucer, the leading reformer in the city, was a man of toleration. At various times the city played host to Andrew Karlstadt, Michael Sattler, Pilgram Marpeck, Melchior Hoffman, Hans Denck, Wilhelm Reublin and Sebastian Franck, all of whom had a part to play in the Anabaptist ferment.

Schwenckfeld opened up debate with Zwingli on the issue of infant baptism, setting out forty six propositions against infant baptism. Schwenckfeld was concerned for the inner transformation of people. For him what mattered was not necessarily the externals, and in that he disagreed with some Anabaptists, but the changed lives within the gathered church.

The teachings of Schwenckfeld, Denck and Franck may have given inspiration in a later age to the Christian Spiritualist movement and are not quite so central to our discussion as those who might be termed evangelical Anabaptists.

The Anabaptists in Hesse

In Hesse, Anabaptist life emerged out of the social tensions of the Peasants' War. It started in an anti-clerical movement, and the first significant leader was Melchior Rinck, once a follower of Thomas Müntzer. The movement developed and Melchior Hoffman gained a considerable following, becoming the dominating influence during the 1530s. Anabaptists flourished in Hesse mainly because of the tolerance of Philip, Landgrave of Hesse, a tolerance which continued through his four sons and heirs. They resisted the death penalty for dissenters.

The Netherlands

In Holland there developed a major controversy over the nature of communion, as part of the general climate of reform. Into this setting came Melchior Hoffman with teaching that, at first glance, appeared to offer an attractive and simpler form of Eucharist. In northern Germany and in Holland the early years of Anabaptist development were marred by events in the town of Münster. Here a group of Anabaptists, led by Jan Matthijs of Haarlem and Jan Beukelz of Leiden, again influenced by the radical idealism of Hoffman and the claims being made for the Peasants, gained control of the city council proclaiming a 'Kingdom of the Elect'.

Two young ladies executed in the bishopric of Bamberg in 1550

A major reshaping of the government of the town ensued, using the teaching of the Old Testament as a mandate. Polygamy was introduced, capital punishment became the norm for even minor legal infringements. The Catholic Bishop besieged the city with troops and captured the city, massacring the inhabitants. The cages which once held the remains of the Anabaptist leaders still hang from the spire of St Lambert's Church in the city. This was and is a sorry tale for the Christian Church, both Catholic and Anabaptist.

The Anabaptists in the region recovered under the leadership of Menno Simmons (1496-1561). He and Dirk Philips rejected the violence of these events as an aberration of the Radical Reformation, and sought to draw out some of the deeper and more spiritual insights of the Anabaptist vision, the development of peaceful communities of gathered believers and the accent on servant discipleship. This is perhaps best illustrated in the story of Dirk Willems of Asperen in Holland. Willems was arrested in 1569 for being an Anabaptist. One day he discovered his cell door open and escaped. He was chased by his gaoler and whilst crossing some frozen water his pursuer fell through the ice. Willems returned to rescue the gaoler. He was re-arrested, imprisoned, tortured and finally subjected to a lingering death by fire on the instructions of the Duke of Alba, Fernando Alvarez de Toledo, Count of Holland, acting under the orders of the Catholic King Philip of Spain.

Jakob Hutter (?-1536)

Jakob Hutter gave his name to one Anabaptist group, the Hutterites of Moravia. They developed a very distinctive form of Christian community life and a community of goods. The Hutterites began in Nikolsberg in Moravia in 1528 under the leadership of Jakob Wiedemann. Jakob Hutter later developed the concept of the economic community of goods, which has become the distinctive mark of the Hutterites, or Bruderhof, in succeeding centuries. It was an attempt to live out the theological understanding that community comes before self in the new order of God. Perhaps it was an insight gained through the peasants' movement which in time became a passionate conviction about justice for poor people. They sent out hundreds of missionaries across Europe, many of whom were martyred. Four hundred and fifty years later Hutterite communities, practising a communitarian lifestyle, are to be found in north America and in the United Kingdom.

A Scriptural, radical, just and peaceful movement

Whatever their contemporaries sought to record, and however mainstream Church history has told the tale, a careful and reflective analysis reveals a picture of a widespread movement in the radical Anabaptist tradition across central and western Europe. The 1500s, marked the desire to gather communities of believers, identified through baptism on their profession of faith, engaged in serious community study of the Scriptures using the Gospels as the key to understanding. There was a deep concern for justice and peace in a relationship where no hierarchy ruled and where the communties did not believe their faith and their understanding of church were subject to the whims of princes, magistrates and rulers, but where the crown rights of the Redeemer prevailed. These were the Anabaptists.

Thomas Müntzer (c1489-1525)

The other so-called Anabaptist everyone remembers, apart from the group in Münster, is Thomas Müntzer. He was born in Stolberg in the Harz Mountains and received a fine education at the Universities of Leipzig and Frankfurt, graduating in theology. He became a priest and after serving as provost of a monastery and pastor of a convent he became preacher at the Church of St Mary in Zwickau in 1520. There he collaborated with the so-called Zwickau prophets in envisioning a spiritualist society in which the peasants would control and lead the church. Christopher Rowland suggests we have a warped knowledge of Müntzer. However, many Anabaptist scholars, whilst noting his radical insights, doubt if he can strictly be counted as an Anabaptist. Some scholars classify him as a Spiritualist. He was in the habit of occasionally publishing pamphlets, one of which Conrad Grebel in Zurich read. He moved around south Germany and Switzerland. The reformer Bullinger assumed there was contact between Müntzer and Grebel as he thought through his Anabaptist proposals in Zurich. A letter exists from Grebel to Müntzer in 1524. The link is that of a radical reformer, but Müntzer died before the distinctive shapes of Anabaptism - believers' baptism, the gathered church etc - could emerge.

English Anabaptists?

Very early on Anabaptist ideas travelled to England. Indeed, the earlier teachings of John Wyclif were one of the pre-Reformation sources that had a place as a building block in the Anabaptist vision. In the first generation of radical reform there was no defined group of people called

Anabaptists. The name was applied by others to almost any group which moved beyond the thinking of the Magisterial Reformers and developed radical ideas around the concept of individuals being free to gather to worship God. This was often linked to an anti-clericalism, a view that you were not born into membership of a particular national church, but you were free to choose for yourself, and that Scripture, rather than tradition, was the norm, the principal reference point for determining the content of Christianity, the pattern of the church and the lifestyle of the believer and of the community.

So, Christopher Hill and others have certainly seen various groups within the radical end of the English Reformation as being Anabaptist. Within the patterns of the groups already looked at, that appears to be a reasonable description. As Hill comments -

> The essential doctrine of Anabaptism was that infants should not be baptized. Acceptance of baptism - reception into the church - should be the voluntary act of an adult. This clearly subverted the concept of a national church to which every English man and woman belonged: it envisaged instead the formation of voluntary congregations by those who believed themselves to be the elect.... Many Anabaptists refused to swear oaths, since they objected to a religious ceremony being used for judicial purposes, others rejected war and military service.

By these criteria, according to Hill, the radical communities which emerged during the English reformation and the Civil War and Commonwealth period, included many Anabaptists. Some went under distinctive names and lasted through several generations. Others, as on the European mainland, involved only one community of people and lasted for only a few years, or developed into a group we now know by a different name.

In an open definition of first generation Anabaptists certain radical groups of the English Reformation deserve consideration as being proto-Anabaptists, or close companions to the Anabaptist vision. For instance, there were the Familists, led in England by Christopher Vittels, who were reported as being numerous in the Diocese of Ely in 1584, an essentially lay movement drawing ideas from Henry Niclaes, born in Münster in 1502.

Again, there was the development of the Leveller and True Leveller, or Digger, movements in the 1640s, concerned for justice for the poor and agrarian reform. Their key thinker, Gerrard Winstanley, was perhaps more politically aware than others, but those involved imbibed a heady mix of theology and concern for social and political justice which grew out of the radical reformation of the Anabaptists.

Tony Benn, addressed a meeting in Burford Churchyard in Oxfordshire in 1976, to commemorate the anniversary of the execution in 1649 of three English soldiers. These men were killed for being members of the Leveller Community. Benn drew attention to the rich Biblical tradition and the local congregational model of Christian community which such groups espoused, a point he once made to a fringe meeting of the Baptist Assembly in the 1980s when he paid tribute to his own Congregational inheritance. This was the world which later bred Milton and Bunyan, a world where religion and politics for a while were part of a sustained radical questioning in closer proximity than we generally espouse; a world where it is unwise to read back too many of our own preconceptions, but rather to see that contemporary commentators, Bishops, Kings and Parliament understood one potent ingredient to be the Anabaptist insights which formed a distinct strand of the Reformation era.

Were there other Anabaptists?

It is Münster that people always recall when they think of the Anabaptists, but it is one small part of a wider story.

Here, we concentrate on the creative points in the testimony of Menno Simmons and his friends, such as the remarkable Dirk Willems. We reflect on the experience of the first Anabaptist congregations, the insights of Hubmaier and the Schleitheim Confession, and keep before us the legacy that was shared across Europe and influenced our own early believers' church. We might think of these groups as evangelical Anabaptists, a normative group for our exploration. Many groups had the title "Anabaptist" applied to them by others - it was, after all, a term of abuse.

Amongst others there are consistent themes about the use of Scripture, the importance of personal response and baptism as a believer, the nature of the church and the missionary dimension which have a relevance for today.

The Reformation Reality

The Anabaptist vision was clearly different from the Magisterial Reform. In this generation scholars from within the tradition have sought to make clear that they are a different, more radical strand of the Reformation, outside the mainstream Protestant developments associated with nation states in the Reformed (Presbyterian), Lutheran and Anglican traditions and those forms of Christianity derived from them such as Methodism. The Anabaptist/Baptist community was persecuted by both Protestant and Catholic churches and states. What perhaps threatened their groupings was the Anabaptist insistence that church and state should be separate and that Europe was not the Christian civilisation that many assumed it to be.

Such a vision undermined the pattern of society that Luther, Zwingli and Calvin, for all their zeal to reform the church, still wished to maintain. In these circumstances Catholic and Protestant united in hatred and persecution of the Anabaptists. It became a term to be avoided and, in part, one which only in our own time has been rescued to be seen afresh as having a compelling vision of the people of God. The Anabaptists understood themselves as being gathered by God and, in a true servant mission, sought to be his disciples in the world.

IV   ANABAPTIST ISSUES

The Anabaptist movement was a radical arm of the Reformation which does not properly belong with the mainstream understanding of Protestantism. The "believers' church" tradition will not fit neatly alongside the Magisterial Reformation of Luther, Zwingli, Calvin and the Anglican Divines. This point has been argued in the years since the Reformation, and the contemporary exploration of this issue is marked by the work of the north American Baptist scholar, James William McClendon Jnr, who has articulated this in his important Systematic Theology, to which we will turn in due course.

It is also my thesis that Anabaptist ideas, in the form we discover them and away from the extreme and regrettable incidents where Anabaptists succumbed to violence and sought to obtain controlling civil power, had an influence upon a whole family of Christian groups. They are a legitimate part of our heritage and, more importantly, bear closer examination today as we seek to develop ourselves to be an authentic radical and missionary community of disciples.

Any two people examining the records of the early Anabaptist groups will come to differing conclusions about what may be regarded as significant emphases and distinctives. However, in the subsequent generations certain key themes have emerged which can be seen to follow from the principal concerns of the first seventy years. To these might be added a selection of sub-themes which certain people have found distinctive and interesting. These sub-themes have generally been identified because they can be seen in some way or other to be drawn from principal issues.

In setting out these concerns I have deliberately mixed some ideas with which Baptists are familiar and which are regarded as part of Baptist heritage, with others which may come to us afresh. There is no strict hierarchy of these ideas save, perhaps, the accent on a Christocentric understanding of Scripture and the Gospel which we discover within it. The randomness of the order, then, is hopefully a challenge to our own thinking and possible complacency.

On being radical

Throughout the first three chapters of this booklet we have looked at what I have described as the Radical Reformation. Radical is an oft-used and oft-misunderstood word. In the context of Anabaptist reflection it is about going to the root of issues; of being as thorough as we can in seeking to get to the fundamentals. The Anabaptists split with Zwingli because he started on a journey he failed to complete. He sought, in the Prophezei school, to uncover the root message of the Bible. With others he wanted to see the key ideas and shape of the New Testament church as best they could be understood through the mists of history and all the complications of exegesis. When it came to what others saw as the New Testament model of the gathered church separated from the state, formed from believers who had made a free and mature response to the Gospel of Jesus Christ, the reforming zeal of Zwingli faltered. The Anabaptists wanted to assert that the truths of Jesus they discerned from the Bible had authority in the shaping not only of the doctrine of the faith, but the nature and shape of the church - ecclesiology - and also the pattern and lifestyle of the believing community - ethical practices. These things were not always seen to be the case when the going got tough. The Magisterial Reformers held back from this approach to understanding the message of Scripture. Anabaptists were known as "root and branch" people - true radicals.

If we are to be like our Anabaptist foreparents we have to be committed to the search for renewal which involves seeking to strip away many of the accretions of tradition and look for the roots of faith and belief. Radicalism has that questing spirit which is not content to take the assumptions of others, to hold to recent practice as the norm which determines what we should do, but rather, though recognising the difficulties, longs to be challenged afresh by a faith which holds to the most primitive and accurate New Testament realities we can uncover. Of course, as we reckon with the incarnation, we will not be foolish enough to search for some distilled pure form of Christianity, without any encumbrance of the historical actualities of first-century Palestine. Yet we will not be content with a twentieth-century faith, which like an old chapel pew, has attracted in the passing of the years, layer after layer of brown varnish so that the original beauty of the wood is lost from sight.

Are we radical people - looking for a church formed out of the New Testament insights? What "traditions" do we put in the way?

A church of the marginalised

From the earliest centuries, the Christian faith has been married to the power of the state. Christendom, arising from that fusion between the Roman Empire and the Orthodox Catholic Church, has been a tool of princes and potentates. The marriage survived the split between west and east, was integral to the Byzantine Empire and to the Holy Roman Empire. Emperors relied upon Popes and Patriarchs for validity and vice versa. The Magisterial Reformation needed political legitimacy, and for Henry VIII the Anglican Reformation met his political needs.

Anabaptists stood apart from all of that. Except for the aberrations of Münster, the Anabaptist vision understands the Gospel to be demonstrating a dynamic form of gathering of believers, free from the power and influence of any earthly ruler, covenanted together as believing communities, answerable only to King Jesus and affirming the crown rights of the Redeemer.

Essentially, these movements have broken out amongst people not at the heart of the social and political world. Rather, mirroring the reality of the early church, the community of faith has been seen as having an appeal and a place for the marginalised. Of course, it is not to deny the Gospel to those of power and influence in the secular world, but it is to indicate they do not have a special place within the church. The Sermon on the Mount sets the tone for those who are being gathered as disciples into the believing family.

There have been times when Baptists have forgotten this. Where we exist in large numbers, where we have the attention of the crowd, we have been as much in danger of using power as other parts of the church - to side with the Kings rather than the Prophets.

Yet the Anabaptist vision draws us in another way. The heart of what we are about is found in the mission of God. We do not lack ideas and concerns for the transformation of society (some of those will be explored later), but we are concerned about the method - for that is part of the message. The Anabaptist vision eschews power for its own sake. It takes a deliberate walk away from the trappings of the nation state, from the opportunity to coerce or dictate, and seeks, rather, in gathering communities of faith to be salt to savour society. The underground living stream is more to our natural way of operating, than the proud city set upon a hill with all the accoutrements of establishment.

Are we a church of the marginalised? Do we look for status, for media access, to be at the heart of civil society, or are we striving to be the servant community of Christ?

Working with the Bible

From the first Prophezei School in Zurich, the use of the Bible amongst Anabaptists has been very important. For a start, they did not give a major role to tradition as Catholic, Orthodox and Anglican scholarship did, though there was an acknowledgment that the Holy Spirit had been at work within the history of the church. Anabaptists did not place an emphasis on a very defined and regulated doctrine, as Calvinism might be said to have done. Rather, emphasis is placed on working as communities of faith with the testimony of the Bible, seeking to quarry our discipleship, our lifestyle, from Jesus as we understand him revealed through Scripture. This does not make us narrow biblicists or caught in one of the many theological debates about the theology of inspiration of scripture. That is a somewhat different point. For Anabaptists it was done in community. There were, as we have seen, scholars in that community, but it was not clericalist. The whole people of God engaged in understanding the Bible, not just the ordained.

For the central tradition of evangelical Anabaptists the New Testament was the starting point and particularly the life and teaching of Jesus. That is a contrast with the way parts of the Magisterial Reformation and, indeed, subsequent Baptist life developed, with a strong emphasis on the letters of Paul. Of course, all Scripture is inspired and worthy of careful study as the Word of God, but a certain "Christocentrism" was the hallmark of the early Anabaptists and provided the key as to how they looked at the whole of Scripture. This emphasis on the life and teaching of Jesus as a hermeneutical key for interpreting the rest of the Old and New Testaments was far reaching and at the heart of the Anabaptist vision. It might be contrasted with Martin Luther who had as a key the writings of Paul - Paulocentrism.

Balthasar Hubmaier took the view that all Scripture pointed to Christ and Anabaptists used Christ as the key to understanding the faith. Such an approach is different to seeing the Bible as a flat whole, as some Reformers did, drawing their ethics and ecclesiology not from a perspective shaped by the life and teaching of Jesus, but from, say, the Old Testament.

On the issue of baptism, for instance, there are those who have built theologies for infant baptism on the back of the Old Testament practice of circumcision, rather than starting with the action and teaching of Jesus in the New.

The Anabaptist insight is not to be sidetracked into the nature of the pattern of inspiration, but rather to ask in our Baptist community "is the life and teaching of Jesus the core which shapes our understanding of scripture and of the faith?"

A simple test might be to look at twelve months of house group programmes or Sunday morning preaching and worship themes. Is the controlling indicator the Gospels? All too often the answer will come back, "no".

The evangelical Anabaptist emphasis could be crucial for us now.

What is your hermeneutical key to the new testament? To which "purple passages" do you turn as you seek to follow Christ?

A gathering church

Here is a core insight from the Anabaptists which we claim to understand well and place at the heart of Free Church and Baptist principles. But do we really? The conviction is that the Gospel is announced and God by His Holy Spirit calls women and men into gathering communities of believers, where all have an important part to play. This gathering church is created by the process of conversion. It is not, of course, simply a pre-existing body moulded by the apostolic experience which those in later generations are invited to join. The Pauline image of the Body of Christ suggests that if any believer in the gathering community fails to take on their due tasks and responsibilities, the life and work of the whole body is put at jeopardy.

I quite deliberately write about a "gathering church" in order to emphasise this is not a complete body of Christ, but a dynamic group of believers, to whom the Triune God continues to add by His Grace. The normal phrase we use is the "gathered" church, but that has the sense of completeness, arrival, about it. Anabaptists saw themselves as being gathered together for a journey of discipleship.

This is a powerful vision of the church. It puts to one side the notion of some who are specially called out and of a different order to others, though it allows plenty of room for those with different gifts, who have their gifts used appropriately, to make the Body work effectively. All too often we take that in a contemporary way to mean everyone can have a say and a vote, but some can do the work.

The gathering church has a sense of community about it. Those being gathered have not opted to join because they like the music, or the preacher has nice hair. No, God has called them into community. In such a situation the contemporary "supermarket" style of Christianity is a long way removed from the Anabaptist model. The gathering church is clearly defined - called to belong - it is clear who is involved. It no doubt raises questions about how large a community can be to support the sense of being a body in community. Are Anabaptists naturally unable to conceive of the large gatherings of people as being a true "believers' church"? It also throws up questions about decision-making. Anabaptists were not democrats. Rather, they looked for the discernment of the will of Christ in their worship, their prayer and conversing.

In the contemporary church we often find a dissatisfaction with a Free Church model which tends to look for making decisions by a mock-Parliament debate and a vote. Some then opt to escape this by looking for others to make the decision; as one new church leader once quipped "swopping a Pope in Rome for a Pope at home." It can lead to a casualness about belonging. Early Baptist communities had more of the Anabaptist sense of discipline. Bound together in the church we have a responsibility one for another. The discipline is not to be handed out by some external authority - the church courts and councils of the Reformed, or a special category of priest, as with Episcopalian models. Rather, it is the whole community watching and waiting with one another - and that needs a developed sense of the love of God as well as His justice.

So, the gathering church talks and listens, searches for the mind of Christ in the clear leading of the community, is concerned for the peace of the body and therefore engages in reflection and prayer which is communal and consultative, rather than confrontational and coercive.

Is the current malaise of the church meeting and the increasing pattern of churches and ministers coming to grief caused by taking too much of a secular political model for the life of the gathering community, rather than this consultative community? Who can tell? But the Anabaptists have a challenge for us.

Is there a limit to the size of a gathering church? Does it cease to be effective if the disciples cannot watch and wait with one another because they do not know one another?

A distinctive lifestyle

Anabaptist groups were soon acknowledged, even by their critics, to live lives which sought to show the marks and pattern of Christ. Of course, the basic marks of that were in the developed personal lifestyle and ethics of the individual believer. We have already seen incidents such as the fascinating tale of Dirk Willems who saved his pursuer from death by drowning, only to suffer rearrest and death by burning for his Anabaptist beliefs.

The story of Dirk Willems has been a very powerful one for people in succeeding generations. James C Juhnke, a north American Mennonite, wrote a powerful short play about the incident, which was first performed in Kansas in 1992. The events are recorded in the Martyrs' Mirror where van Braght comments -

> *In the year 1569 a pious, faithful brother and follower of Jesus Christ, named Dirk Willems, was apprehended in Asperen, Holland, and had to endure severe tyranny from the papists.... when he fled he was hotly pursued by a thief-catcher, and as there had been some frost, (the) said Dirk Willems ran before over the ice, getting across with considerable peril. The thief-catcher, following him, broke through, when Dirk Willems, perceiving that former was in danger of his life, quickly returned and aided him getting out, and thus saved his life. The thief-catcher wanted to let him go, but the burgomaster very sternly called by him to consider his oath.*

The town records of Asperen show that Dirk, aged somewhere between fifteen and twenty, was baptized as a believer in Rotterdam and met with others in worship in Asperen. The Judges at his trial ordered him to be executed with fire until death and all his property be confiscated because of his Anabaptist beliefs.

Truth telling, declining to take an oath, but regarding it as a matter of discipleship to speak the truth, was one mark of Anabaptists which has a very contemporary challenge. The Reformers wanted to purge all oath-taking, except an oath in God. This did not happen and nowadays throughout the legal system and in many aspects of society people are expected to take an oath. Anabaptists abolished all of that. In our own land those other radical reformers, the Quakers, have kept true to this part of the vision and are noted for their honesty - let your "yes" be" yes" and your "no" be "no"; whereas, contemporary society might be noted for its deceit.

In his inaugural lecture as Director of the Centre for Christianity and Culture at Regents Park College, Oxford, in 1996, the Mennonite scholar, Alan Kreider, asked "is it possible to be truth tellers in a society where lying is now a way of life?" As the Advices and Queries of the Society of Friends puts it -

> *Are you honest and truthful in all you say and do? Do you maintain strict integrity in business transactions and in your dealings with organisations? Do you use your money and information entrusted to you with discretion and responsibility? Taking oaths implies a double standard of truth; in choosing to affirm instead, be aware of the claim to integrity that you are making.*

Early Anabaptist communities practised a total community of goods. Whilst most did retain personal ownership of property, all were clear that their possessions were not their own and should be readily available to help those in need. Hutterite communities still practice this style of communal living and sharing. In a world where we have seen secular pressure very much on the acquiring of personal possessions, is there not a case for reflecting, for the good of the whole inhabited earth, whether holding things in common, sharing transport, pooling manufactured consumer goods, is not the sort of lifestyle which would make us more Christ-like in our stewardship of this created world?

The developing of a style of living for Christ which is open and transparent, marked by a desire to follow the Sermon on the Mount, is a frightening challenge. Yet it was that Christocentrism we have already remarked upon which placed Anabaptists in a special category.

As the old question has it - "if you were arrested for being a Christian, would there be enough evidence to convict you"? Anabaptists take lifestyle issues seriously - discipleship is more than going to church on a Sunday and not buying a lottery ticket. What are the Christlike distinctives of your life?

An inclusive community

The very nature of the Anabaptist understanding saw women and men being gathered into the believers' church without gender or rank being a concern. The distinct anti-clericalism of the Anabaptist communities ensured that when someone was understood as being admitted into a particular covenanted group the gifts they brought were there for the strengthening of the priesthood of all believers.

That immediately dispenses with the need for a special priestly or pastor class, and in this they moved beyond the models of ordered ministry which became marks of the Magisterial Reformation. They did not reject those who could enable the gathering church to grow and reflect together - it was not anti-intellectual in any simple sense. Rather, the insight draws us towards looking for those who can enable the church community to develop discipleship. Servant ministry becomes the premium, rather than authoritarian leadership.

And whilst the point took some time to flower fully, from the beginning women found a greater freedom within Anabaptist communities than in society as a whole. Many women took a central role in gathering churches. Not a few were martyred for their beliefs. Maeyken Boosers, a Belgian mother of several children, was imprisoned for her Anabaptist beliefs. She was tortured on the rack and, refusing to give up her beliefs, was burned to death in 1564. Her fate was sealed when she declared -

> My heart constantly longs to be fit in His sight, that I might finish to His praise that which He has commenced in me.

Both women and men were early martyrs of the Anabaptist cause and the gifts and insights of all gathered into the community were treasured. In early Anabaptist communities women served as prophets, evangelists, in leading prayer and sharing in the tasks of mutual aid. That issue is one the contemporary church struggles with. The accent on the Pauline doctrinal points and the Old Testament priestly caste, draws us away from the place that Jesus gave to women in the Gospels.

The gathering communities established by Anabaptists were built, as is now clear, around a concept of koinonia where women and men understood their primary relationships as being that of sisters and brothers in the Lord. From this understanding followed their perspectives on marriage; perspectives which were radical in their outworking, affecting the whole understanding of Christian marriage.

This is a contemporary Anabaptist challenge to the powerful patriarchies that all too often lay down what the church will be, and fail to accept the contribution of women.

For women it is an especial challenge, as Ruth Gouldbourne has creatively argued in her 1997 Whitley Lecture. Do women have to find ways of seeking to bring their gifts to the life of the Christian community by engaging with the patriarchy, or is there a case, as some have argued, for another model of church, a radical women's church; a church community where the insights of women determine the shape of the community which believers can join?

In any event, the Anabaptist vision throws open to churches the challenge. Are we truly a gathering church of women and men, young and old, where the enabling servant ministry of all is valued and used on a Gospel model, or are we caught in a patriarchal fix which Christendom gave us and which the Reformers never quite reformed?

The questioning throws up a challenge about ministry. It ought, on an Anabaptist model, to be a servant, enabling ministry and not a dominant leadership ministry. There are disturbing issues here; for instance, is it right to use the titles "Pastor" and "Reverend" ?

The Anabaptists, it should be noted, were not anti-intellectual. Hubmaier and others were great scholars, but their contribution was put alongside that of others, weighed and reflected on in the gathering of the church, not accepted from on high as pronouncements from a person of superior caste.

Sixty per cent of Baptist church members are women. Is that reflected in the leadership of the churches, the associations and the Union? Are we not still, as Ruth Gouldbourne claims, caught with a male patriarchy?

An ecumenical church

Anabaptists were inclusive people, not in the sense of deciding all who lived in a certain place were part of the church, as national and folk churches are wont to do in the parish system; rather, in not being caught by the link with a nation state, which determines boundaries, or seeing an exclusiveness of approach - we are right and everyone else is wrong - which is the mark of some of the great confessional families. John Howard Yoder has argued that Anabaptists were the first true ecumenists, which might come as a surprising view to many.

Yoder argues -

> *Alone of all the churches of the Reformation they were truly international. Not only did they maintain contact all the way from England to Macedonia, but with their rejection of the state church and of war they broke down the greatest barriers to Christian fellowship which have operated in modern times.*

Anabaptists argued that the church is essentially missionary, unhindered by what is a relatively recent development, the concept of the nation state. Of course, Baptists have generally fallen into the trap in later centuries of determining their wider associating by reference to civil government, but it is not natural to the Anabaptist heritage so to do. There is a proper argument for saying that to be a Christian according to "Anabaptist orthodoxy", is not a matter of belonging to the right Christian world communion, nor of signing up to any particular denominational confessional creed - the Thirty Nine Articles of the Anglican Communion, the Augsburg confession or the like - but rather of orthopraxies. By that I mean holding fast in a local gathering church of believers to a Christocentric view of Scripture; being committed to the concept of the gathering church; holding fast with a Biblical model of Baptism and to the gathering community being the place for determining the mind of Christ and handling the disciplining of the faithful. All this to be done where there is a vision of associating with other like-minded gathering communities.

Yoder and others have argued it is a high priority for such gathered faithful communities to seek to establish and maintain true koinonia - community with others who confess Christ. As he says -

they require not only polite mutual recognition or even "intercommunion".... if there is to be a breach in fellowship between us that breach cannot be our initiative.

So the Anabaptist gathering church is a dynamic community working together with others at hearing the voice of Jesus in the Bible and then going and living that out in society.

Are we wrong to associate with others on geographic or narrow confessional grounds alone? Are we not called to be true ecumenists and internationalists, unencumbered by ideas of nationhood and working with all those who name the name of Jesus and seek to be His true disciples?

Freedom of religion and human rights

It was Thomas Helwys who, having discovered something of the Anabaptist vision as he met up with Menno Simons and his followers, expounded most clearly the call for religious freedom as a basic human right. The Anabaptist vision has always sought after that, not only for those who belong to the radical reformation, but other faith communities, Christian and others. Helwys, addressing King James I of England (King James IV of Scotland) in 1612 wrote -

Let them be heretics, Turks, Jews, or whatsoever, it appertains not to the earthly power to punish them in the least measure....mens religion is betwixt God and themselves.

That great claim fits clearly within the Anabaptist vision. The moment you insist that faith is a matter which is separate from the country of which you are a citizen; that people are being freely called into communities of belief, is the moment the application of freedom to believe or not must be taken seriously.

These points of faith have been enshrined in the contemporary world in such documents as the United Nations Declaration of Human Rights, the Constitution of the United States of America, in the Helsinki accords of the Organisation for Security and Cooperation in Europe. There is an International Court of Human Rights established in the Netherlands - the very country where Helwys reflected on these issues in the early 1600s. Yet the sad truth is that such rights are denied in many parts of the world and Baptists have often failed to champion them. They remain our strong desire - but that desire has to be for others, as well as ourselves.

We argue for the rights of Christian believers in other countries and seek to protect our own, but are we still concerned for the human rights of those with whom we disagree? Who are they? What should we be doing to protect them, as well as ourselves?

Peacemaking

Though some remember Anabaptists as violent people because of the incident referred to earlier, the great centre of the movement was made up of women and men of peace, who rejected violence, did not carry weapons, refused to go to war against other human beings or to defend themselves by force. For them the teaching of the Sermon on the Mount was very important. "Blessed are the peacemakers" was to be taken very seriously. This insight was marked particularly by Menno Simons and those who came after him.

Wayne Pipkin, a noted Anabaptist scholar, says of him -

> He preached by night to secret conventicles and baptized new believers in streams and out-of-the way lakes. He established churches and ordained pastors throughout northern Europe. He sought to prove that the extremist example of Münster was atypical of Anabaptists... Menno underscored the principle that followers of Christ were non-violent and did not practice vengeance. The way of the Christian disciple was different from those who were not.

That peacemaking model has been true to many descendants of the Radical Reformation. It is not a passive vision, but an active lifestyle. It caused many of the first generation, like Dirk Willems, to face death. In contemporary peace-churches - Mennonites, the Society of Friends and others, inheritors of that Anabaptist vision - it has led to reflection on non-violent resistance to powers and principalities, to the development of mediation and reconciliation ministries, whose contemporary value goes far beyond the communities which practice both peacemaking and non-violent change.

In our own time there have been Baptists who have sought to ask what insights we may gain from reflection on what it might be to become a peace-church. The Baptist Peace Fellowship issued a challenge to the Baptist Union to consider this possibility during the Denominational Consultation of 1996. Reflection on that call continues. Paul Dekar, in his excellent book on Baptist peacemakers, helps identify the Baptist legacy in this tradition. He comments -

> *Among the radical ideas put forward by the followers of Smythe was the conviction that they should follow the unarmed and unweaponed cross-bearing footsteps of Jesus. As a result, early Baptists ensured that peacemaking was securely part of the Baptist heritage even though the Baptist denomination did not become one of the historic peace churches.*

Dekar is right, but his book bears testimony to the many in the peace-churches and in the Baptist tradition who have been challenged by the Sermon on the Mount and have sought to follow the cross-bearing footsteps of Jesus. Whatever else history has taught us, to be a peacemaker is no easy option, but it is a witness to Christ.

How do I react to the peace church testimony? What has been the influence of those, like Ghandi and Martin Luther King Jnr, who led movements for non-violent change? Do I feel content with theories of the "just war"?

Missionary congregations

Anabaptists, by their very nature, had a story to tell and to live based on the Christ they encountered in the Gospels. These days it is commonplace to assume that every part of the Christian family is committed to being a mission-focused community engaged in the evangelisation of the world. The methods change, the emphasis of traditions are markedly different, but there is a common assumption.

That may be true. The Anabaptists, however, from the earliest days have borne a particular emphasis towards mission, which is rooted in other insights. Mission is the nature of the gathering community. As we have seen, it is not the prerogative of some - a special class or group; it is the responsibility of all. It is not only about words, but intrinsically about a servant lifestyle and deeds. It is a freely offered dimension to faith and can be accepted or rejected, though the impulse is always to want to share the truth. The British Baptist lay theologian, Haddon Willmer, comments

> *The Sermon on the Mount...has repeatedly disturbed customary Western Christianity in this century and I trust it will do so again. It calls for perfection modelled on the Father in heaven, ethics without compromise, faith in God without anxiety, openness of being without hypocritical exhibitionism, love of enemies. It presents Jesus saying among other things: Do not be anxious about tomorrow, for tomorrow will be anxious for itself (Matt 6.34).*

What we need for the future are churches that encourage choosers - people willing to act radically and take responsibility. The contemporary debate on missionary congregations might have been intended for evangelical Anabaptists! The core values of such missionary congregations will be very important and we note that there has been work done on identifying core values of justice for Baptist communities in our own times. Of course, the point is not to debate it, or strategise about it, but to go and do it.

Have we come to terms with being the body of Christ in this contemporary age? Is mission aimed at building true human community at the heart of our own agenda?

The baptism of believers only

Out of the concerns of a gathering church, drawn together in a missionary congregation, reflecting together on the insights of Scripture, the first Anabaptists came to the conclusion which gave rise to the name by which others knew them. Though they had been baptized in infancy into the Catholic church, baptism as a believer seemed to be more authentic to the Gospel, as the grace of the Triune God made that known to them.

Today, the baptism of believers is a key concept. It is an action that involves an individual, a gathering community and God. No one can baptize themselves. It is a community activity. Baptism is not isolated from the action of God, nor from incorporation into a gathering community. Many Baptists have an inadequate view of baptism at this point. Far too many churches leave it to a minister to decide who will be baptized. In many communities baptism takes place without any commitment to belonging to a gathering community of faith. Such baptism is less than believers' baptism. It deserves the title sometimes given to it by others - adult baptism.

The nature of the baptismal initiation process is an area of much contemporary debate by Baptists and in ecumenical circles. The issues raised in two books, *Believing and Being Baptised* and *Reflections on the Water* are well worth pursuing.

Do we truly understand the baptismal reality? Are we short-changing people when we allow baptism without the covenant to a gathering community of believers?

The Separation of Church and State

Anabaptists rejected all coercion in matters of faith. As we have seen, the Magisterial Reformers kept clear the link between the rule of the Magistrate, whether as Godly prince, or Town council, and the church. Anabaptists sought to separate the two. This argument about separation can become sterile and strange in some settings, but our own history points to the disadvantages we have suffered as those who have not been linked to the apparatus of the State. In many countries today there is a link between a national or state church and the government which places other communities of faith at a disadvantage and can often work against the interests of true Christian belief and action in a national church.

In eastern Europe the link is often made that to belong to the national church is to be a good citizen of the country. In England the state church enjoys privileges in the political world and access to government ministers, though it claims to be disadvantaged in terms of the Crown appointing its senior leaders.

Today, many people who in principle agree with the separation of church and state still collude at some instances where the links exist. Are we convinced of this issue? What about the seductive calls that come to participate in the life of the state, or to take advantage of the privileges afforded to a state church?

The Anabaptist vision does not call us to disengage from the real world of the whole of society. However, it does call us to express a prophetic edge, a challenge to those in authority. To do that effectively, we may need to be suitably distanced from the corrupting influences which so easily come as we rely on sharing in the life of the powerful - the powers and principalities of the state.

Do we really believe in being free from the state? What about when we use state funds for our buildings and youth work? Or when we are annoyed that the views of Baptists on important issues do not feature in the media?

A Eucharistic community

The early Anabaptists were people who gathered around the Word and Table. They saw themselves as a sacramental community of faith experiencing the reality of the Risen Christ, not least as they met Him in the Word, confessed Him in Baptism and shared the meal He had called them to share in the Upper Room, on the lakeside and in those moments such as the events in Emmaus.

Baptists have adhered to a Zwinglian Eucharistic theology. At its extreme, we have failed to understand the true teaching of Zwingli. We have certainly missed the rich heritage of Hubmaier and others who had a deep sacramentalism not borne out of long-past philosophical reflections on the nature of matter, the debates about transubstantiation and contransubstantiation, which Roman Catholics and Lutherans engaged in during the Reformation era.

No, for the Anabaptists there was another form of spirituality focused in their Christocentric faith, understanding the gathered community itself as koinonia - communion, with that Eucharistic expression - where two or three are gathered, there Christ is in the midst. That reality is most powerfully expressed when the Word has been broken and then the bread and the cup is shared.

The Anabaptists looked for the real presence of Christ in their midst as they worshipped and shared the meal. Baptists have been in danger of implying they did not perceive Christ present at the meal in an arid and extreme form of Zwinglianism, which Zwingli himself would not have owned.

The gathering around a meal and the recalling of the stories of faith have been at the heart of the Judaeo-Christian tradition. From time to time that deep spiritual experience can be distorted by the imposition of formularies of action, or the handing to one group a special role, which obscures the importance of the remembrance, the memorial. The Anabaptists lived in a time of danger and of expectation. For them the meal together was both a time for recall and a time of anticipation. As I argue elsewhere, Baptists have much to recover in terms of the appreciation of this understanding that we are gathered into a Eucharistic koinonia. We should not be frightened of the sacramentality of the community meal.

What is the Eucharistic practice of your church? The New Testament implies weekly celebration. Anabaptists saw it as a key community gathering around the table. Would you describe your church as a community where the meal is a highlight of worship?

In search of a theology

These Anabaptist insights all have a contemporary relevance. We have no great pattern or guides, nor many examples of baptistic groupings working at these issues in any systematic theological way. Unlike other parts of the Christian world family we appear not to have been good at systematic theology. Yet, there is hope in all this. The contemporary interest in an Anabaptist, or baptistic vision, has its systematizers and champions within theological circles. James William McClendon Jnr is a Baptist in north

America who has done much in our own time to promote a contemporary attempt to systematise a Baptist theology. He lists five insights, which taken together might be said to comprise the key-

> *Biblicism - understood not as one or another theory of inspiration, but as humble acceptance of the authority of Scripture for both faith and practice.*

> *Mission - understood not as an attempt to control history for the ends we believe to be good, but as the responsibility to witness to Christ - and accept the suffering that witness entails*

> *Liberty, or soul competency - understood not as the overthrow of all oppressive authority, but as God-given freedom to respond to God without the intervention of the state or other powers.*

> *Discipleship - understood neither as a vocation for the few nor an esoteric discipline for adepts, but as the life transformed into service by the lordship of Jesus Christ (signified by believers' baptism).*

> *Community - understood not as privileged access to God or to sacred status, but as sharing together in a storied life of obedient service to and with Christ (signified by the Lord's Supper).*

A contemporary Baptist vision

The first Anabaptists raised issues in the Radical Reformation, which were not always thought through in the tumultuous times in which they lived. Some groups continued to explore those ideas in the succeeding centuries, but at various points insights were diluted, or the influence of the Magisterial Reformers came to dominate.

Some of the ideas of these Christocentric people have, it appears to me, a conviction and an interest which calls for further exploration in our own time. The radical roots from which we have come sought to establish gathering communities of faith, outwith the constraints of the nation state and the national church for missionary purposes. Their discipleship at times offers a stark challenge to our own.

V WHERE TO NOW?

We have had a "taster" of the Anabaptist story and the Anabaptist distinctives. Some of these distinctives are clearly being reflected upon with great care and interest in the light of the contemporary missiological task. As you have reflected on the points made you may have become excited to reflect further, to explore and develop a contemporary church mission structure based on Anabaptist principles.

Certain themes - ecclesiology; baptism; the 'free church', over against state church, principle are commonplace in Baptist reflection and identity. Some of the other themes may have a particular relevance to a post-modern culture and a contemporary missiological dimension.

It is my conviction that we need to look seriously at the evangelical Anabaptist ideas, which come out of the time of the Radical Reformation, which are part of our heritage and could well be an important resource for the church to draw on in this post-modern, post-Christendom world. I hope you have been challenged by these insights, from communities who drew their inspiration from a Christocentric understanding of Scripture, who were not afraid to look at the roots of believing and who engaged in exciting exploration of what it might mean to be a gathering believers' church.

The Anabaptists were reacting to both the worst side of the corruptions of the Catholic church and to some of the political trading going on between church and state with the Magisterial Reformers. It is, therefore, wise to be alert to the points where the advocacy of one insight may, in extreme cases, lead to the denial of another legitimate Christian insight or theme.

The championing of a Christocentric approach to Scripture is a proper evangelical Anabaptist perspective. Some contemporary Christians exist on a Pauline diet alone; still others feast only on the books of the law in the Old Testament. A Christocentric bias does not cut out using the whole counsel of God as contained in the Scriptures, but it does provide a hermeneutical key.

The conviction of the value and calling of all into the body of Christ - the infinite worth of each person in the gathering church is a clear insight, but it ought not to lead to where Anabaptists themselves did not go. It should not lead into devaluing or rejecting the enabling role of some individuals who by their gifting, their training and their charisma are able to help the gathering church understand the story of the people of God, the insights of theology and the development of a credible missiology.

The accent on the importance of the gathering church having the responsibility for the life and witness of both the community and the individual within it must not be turned into a narrow and destructive legalism where people are constantly using the discipline of the church to ban one another from participation in the life of the church.

The vision that the church is called out of society has to be emphasised as a positive attribute so that we can be salt and light, and seek, by our lives and our mission, to change society for the better, not to withdraw and abandon society as a lost cause. We must not confuse the emphasis on seeking the mind of Christ together, and not submitting to some hierarchical authority within the church, with separating from those who do not share every minor idea or value. The principle of the gathering churches associating with others and listening to the testimony of others is affirmed again and again in Anabaptist writings.

Yet these cautions expressed, my contention is that there is much of value in the passion, vision and commitment of the radical reformers. To ignore it is to miss out on exciting possibilities for contemporary Christian believing. The Anabaptists, for all their differences, represented in their day a serious attempt to come to terms with the message of the Scriptures understood particularly from a Christocentric perspective, and with an accent upon a gathering church committed to developing a lifestyle and mission which engaged credibly with the surrounding world.

Today, there are distinctive challenges from their story which can be part of our story. Stuart Murray offers these clear challenges in a piece he wrote for *Anabaptism Today* in 1997-

> *take Jesus seriously and do not dilute His teachings or shy away from his "hard sayings".*

build churches which are really nonconformist and free, which encourage discipleship, mutual caring and economic radicalism.

look carefully at issues of power, violence and warfare and how the churches should respond to these.

identify and work for the removal of the vestiges of Christendom - the established church, bishops in the House of Lords, oaths in court, preferential treatment for Christianity

develop a coherent approach to issues of persecution and suffering. Anabaptists regarded suffering as the mark of the true church. Many were imprisoned, tortured, martyred.

In our society, where people are driven apart to sit with pre-packaged meals in their own insulated worlds in front of either the television screen, or the computer surfing the net, the Anabaptist vision draws us back into a true koinonia. This is the reality of a community of commitment, where we know one another and meet to affirm a common covenant to Christ and to each other. A community where word and meal define our lifestyle and where, free from the strictures of the secular authorities, from the rule of princes and potentates, we search together for the mind of Christ. Here the faithful gathering church recognises Christ will take His people out to love and serve the world for which He died.

VI   THE SCHLEITHEIM CONFESSION: THE SEVEN ARTICLES

The key points from the Schleitheim Confession of 1527

The articles we have dealt with, and in which we have been united, are these: baptism, ban, the breaking of bread, separation from abomination, shepherds in the congregation, the sword, the oath.

I   Notice concerning baptism. Baptism shall be given to all those who have been taught repentance and the amendment of life and [who] believe truly that their sins are taken away through Christ, and to all those who desire to walk in the resurrection of Jesus Christ and be buried with Him in death, so that they might rise with Him; to all those who with such an understanding themselves desire and request it from us; hereby is excluded all infant baptism, the greatest and first abomination of the Pope. For this you have the reasons and the testimony of the writings and the practise of the apostles. We wish simply yet resolutely and with assurance to hold to the same.

II   We have been united as follows concerning the ban. The ban shall be employed with all those who have given themselves over to the Lord, to walk after [Him] in His commandments; those who have been baptized into the one body of Christ, and let themselves be called brothers or sisters, and still somehow slip and fall into error and sin, being inadvertently overtaken. The same [shall] be warned twice privately and the third time be publicly admonished before the entire congregation according to the command of Christ (Mt. 18). But this shall be done according to the ordering of the Spirit of God before the breaking of bread so that we may all in one spirit and in one love break and eat from one bread and drink from one cup.

III   Concerning the breaking of bread. We have become one and agree thus: all those who desire to break the one bread in remembrance of the broken body of Christ and all those who wish to drink of one drink in remembrance of the shed blood of Christ, they must beforehand be united in the one body of Christ, that is the congregation of God, whose head is Christ, and that by baptism. For as Paul indicates, we cannot be partakers at the same time of the table of the Lord and the table of devils. Nor can we at the same time partake and drink of the cup of the Lord and the cup of devils. That is: all those who have fellowship with the dead works of darkness have no part in the light. Thus all who follow the devil and the world, have no part with those who have been called out of the world unto God. All those who lie in evil have no part in the good.

So it shall and must be, that whoever does not share the calling of the one God to one faith, to one baptism, to one spirit, to one body together with all the children of God, may not be made one loaf together with them, as must be true if one wishes truly to break bread according to the command of Christ.

IV   We have been united concerning the separation that shall take place from the evil and the wickedness which the devil has planted in the world, simply in this; that we have no fellowship with them, and do not run with them in the confusion of their abominations. So it is: since all who have not entered into the obedience of faith and have not united themselves with God so that they will to do His will, are a great abomination before God, therefore nothing else can or really will grow or spring forth from them than abominable things. Now there is nothing else in the world and all creation than good or evil, believing and unbelieving, darkness and light, the world and those who are [come] out of the world, God's temple and idols, Christ and Belial, and none will have part with the other.

To us, then, the commandment of the Lord is also obvious, whereby He orders us to be and to become separated from the evil one, and thus He will be our God and we shall be His sons and daughters.

Further, He admonishes us therefore to go out from Babylon and from the earthly Egypt, that we may not be partakers in their torment and suffering, which the Lord will bring upon them.

From all this we should learn that everything which has not been united with our God in Christ is nothing but an abomination which we should shun. By this are meant all popish and repopish works and idolatry, gatherings, church attendance, winehouses, guarantees and commitments of unbelief, and other things of the kind, which the world regards highly, and yet which are carnal or flatly counter to the command of God, after the pattern of all the iniquity which is in the world. From all this we shall be separated and have no part with such, for they are nothing but abominations, which cause us to be hated before our Christ Jesus, who has freed us from the servitude of the flesh and fitted us for the service of God and the Spirit whom He has given us.

Thereby shall also fall away from us the diabolical weapons of violence - such as sword, armor, and the like, and all of their use to protect friends or against enemies - by virtue of the word of Christ: "you shall not resist evil."

V   We have been united as follows concerning shepherds in the church of God. The shepherd in the church shall be a person according to the rule of Paul, fully and completely, who has a good report of those who are outside of the faith. The office of such a person shall be to read and exhort and teach, warn, admonish, or ban in the congregation, and properly to preside among the sisters and brothers in prayer, and in the breaking of bread, and in all things to take care of the body of Christ, that it may be built up and developed, so that the name of God might be praised and honoured through us, and the mouth of the mocker be stopped.

He shall be supported, wherein he has need, by the congregation which has chosen him, so that he who serves the gospel can also live therefrom, as the Lord has ordered. But should a shepherd do something worthy of reprimand, nothing shall be done with him without the voice of two or three witnesses. If they sin they shall be publicly reprimanded, so that others might fear.

But if the shepherd should be driven away or led to the Lord by the cross, at the same hour another shall be ordained to his place, so that the little folk and the little flock of God may not be destroyed, but be preserved by warning and be consoled.

VI   We have been united as follows concerning the sword.

The sword is an ordering of God outside the perfection of Christ. It punishes and kills the wicked, and guards and protects the good. In the law the sword is established over the wicked for punishment and for death, and the secular rulers are established to wield the same.

But within the perfection of Christ only the ban is used for the admonition and exclusion of the one who has sinned, without the death of the flesh, simply the warning and the command to sin no more.

Now many, who do not understand Christ's will for us, will ask: whether a Christian may or should use the sword against the wicked for the protection and defence of the good, or for the sake of love.

The answer is unanimously revealed: Christ teaches and commands us to learn from Him, for He is meek and lowly of heart and thus we shall find rest for our souls. Now Christ says to the woman who was taken in adultery, not that she should be stoned according to the law of His Father (and yet He says "what the Father commanded me, that I do") but with mercy and forgiveness and the warning to sin no more, says: "Go, sin no more." Exactly thus should we also proceed, according to the rule of the ban.

Second, is asked concerning the sword: whether a Christian should pass sentence in disputes and strife about worldly matters, such as the unbelievers have with one another. The answer: Christ did not wish to decide or pass judgement between brother and brother concerning inheritance, but refused to do so. So should we also do.

Third, is asked concerning the sword: whether the Christian should be a magistrate if he is chosen thereto. This is answered thus: Christ was to be made king, but He fled and did not discern the ordinance of His Father. Thus we should also do as He did and follow after Him, and we shall not walk in darkness. For He Himself says: "Whoever would come after me, let him deny himself and take up his cross and follow me." He Himself further forbids the violence of the sword when He says; "The princes of this world lord it over them etc. but among you it shall not be so." Further Paul says, "Whom God has foreknown, the same he has also predestined to be conformed to the image of his Son," etc. Peter also says: "Christ has suffered (not ruled) and has left us an example, that you should follow after in his steps."

Lastly one can see in the following points that it does not befit a Christian to be a magistrate: the rule of the government is according to the flesh, that of the Christians according to the spirit. Their houses and dwelling remain in this world, that of the Christians is in heaven. Their citizenship is in this world, that of the Christians is in heaven. The weapons of their battle and warfare are carnal and only against the flesh, but the weapons of Christians are spiritual, against the fortification of the devil. The worldly are armed with steel and iron, but Christians are armed with the armour of God, with truth, righteousness, peace, faith, salvation, and with the Word of God. In sum: as Christ our Head is minded, so also must be minded the members of the body of Christ through Him, so that there be no division in the body, through which it would be destroyed. Since then Christ is as written of Him, so must His members also be the same, so that His Body may remain whole and unified for its own advancement and upbuilding. For any kingdom which is divided within itself will be destroyerd.

VII We have been united as follows concerning the oath.
The oath is a confirmation among those who are quarreling or making promises. In the law it is commanded that it should be done only in the name of God, truthfully and not falsely. Christ, who teaches the perfection of the law, forbids His [followers] all swearing, whether true nor false; neither by heaven nor by earth, neither by Jerusalem nor by our head; and that for the reason which He goes on to give: "For you cannot make one hair white or black." You see, thereby all swearing is forbidden. We cannot perform what is promised in swearing, for we are not able to change the smallest part of ourselves.

Now there are some who do not believe the simple commandment of God and who say, "But God swore by Himself to Abraham, because He was God (as He promised him that He would do good to him and would be his God if he kept His commandments). Why then should I not swear if I promise something to someone?" The answer: hear what Scripture says: "God, since he wished to prove overabundantly to the heirs of His promise that His will did not change, inserted an oath so that by two immutable things we might have a stronger consolation (for it is impossible that God should lie)". Notice the meaning of the passage: God has the power to do what He forbids you, for everything is possible to Him. God swore an oath to Abraham, Scripture says, in order to prove that His counsel is immutable. That means: no one can withstand and thwart His will; thus He can keep His oath. But we cannot, as Christ said above, hold or perform our oath, therefore we should not swear.

Others say that swearing cannot be forbidden by God in the New Testament when it was commanded in the Old, but that it is forbidden only to swear by heaven, earth, Jerusalem, and our head. Answer: hear the Scripture. He who swears by heaven, swears by God's throne and by Him who sits thereon. Observe: swearing by heaven is forbidden, which is only God's throne; how much more is it forbidden to swear by God himself. You blind fools, what is greater, the throne or He who sits upon it?

Others say, if it is then wrong to use God for truth, then the apostles Peter and Paul also swore. Answer: Peter and Paul only testify to that which God promised Abraham, whom we long after have received. But when one testifies, one testifies concerning that which is present, whether it be good or evil. Thus Simeon spoke of Christ to Mary and testified: "Behold: this one is ordained for the falling and rising of many in Israel and to be a sign which will be spoken against."

Christ taught us similarly when He says: Your speech shall be yea, yea; and nay, nay; for what is more than that comes of evil. He says, your speech or your word shall be yes and no, so that no one might understand that He permitted it. Christ is simply yea and nay, and all those who seek Him simply will understand His Word. Amen.

VII GLOSSARY OF TERMS

This Glossary of Terms is given for those unfamiliar with some of the terms used. It gives a brief description of some of the key words and phrases.

Anabaptist. Originally a term of abuse used, along with other phrases such as Catabaptist, to describe individuals and groups who, in the 16th Century, espoused a wide range of Christian doctrines on the importance of individual decision in matters of faith, the right of the church to gather in community and worship Christ according to Scripture and their own discernment, rather than according to the law of the land. For many groups the key point which marked them out was the rejection of infant baptism in favour of the baptism of a believer. Hence, re-baptizer.

Evangelical Anabaptist is used to indicate groups who remained orthodox Trinitarian in their belief and who had a concern for proclamation of the Christian message and evangelisation. Some Anabaptist groups developed unorthodox beliefs with the passage of time.

Baptists fall into two distinct groups in England. The General Baptists, coming out of the group who journeyed to Amsterdam. They were Arminian in theology. Some lapsed into Unitarianism in the 1700s. Others were revitalised in the evangelical revival of the 1700s under the leadership of Dan Taylor and formed the General Baptists of the New Connexion, which united with the Particular Baptists in 1891 to form the Baptist Union, as we know it today.

The Particular Baptists were more Calvinistic in their theology. Some developed a rigid, if not arid, Calvinism in the 1700s and formed the Strict and Particular group of Baptist churches. Others, led by key people such as William Carey and Andrew Fuller, adopted a form of more evangelical Calvinism and united with the General Baptists of the New Connexion in 1891. Some Baptists in the USA today advocate a more strict adherence to the five key tenets of Calvinism.

Consubstantiation was the view of the Eucharistic presence held by Martin Luther. Luther taught, in contrast to Transubstantiation, that the substance of the bread and wine remained but that the substances of Christ's body and blood were respectively united with them.

Diggers, Levellers and True Levellers were groups in the English Reformation period who were generally peasants and who took a radical view of the teachings of Christ and often applied them in practical, but revolutionary ways, as with the establishing of a colony at St. George's Hill, near Cobham in the 1640s.

Eucharist, or Thanksgiving, is one of the key words used to describe the act of worship when we remember the instruction from Christ to recall His life, death and resurrection in a meal. It is used here in place of the Lord's Supper, or Communion, which might be more familiar words to some readers. To receive the Eucharist, or Communion, in both kinds is to receive both the bread and the wine. The practise had grown up in medieval times of only giving the laity the bread and not the wine, in case "the blood of Christ" was spilt.

Familists or Family of Love, taught that heaven and hell were to be found in this world. They might recapture on earth the state of innocence which existed before the fall. Familism was spread in England by Christopher Vittels, an itinerant joiner of Dutch origin.

Gathering church is used in place of the more familiar "gathered church", to describe a community of believers being added to by the Holy Spirit in a dynamic way, where God's grace and the response of believing faith are involved in an active and participatory way.

Koinonia is a transliteration of the New Testament Greek word which has several meanings in English, including fellowship, participation, sharing and communion. It is a key term in much contemporary thinking about the nature of life within the Christian community, as well as being a key word in our understanding of the Eucharist.

Magisterial Reformers describes the three key leaders of the western Reformation, Martin Luther, Huldrych Zwingli and Jean (John) Calvin. The term can also be applied to those who worked with them and developed the Protestant Reformation into the second generation such as Philip Melancthon, Martin Bucer and John Knox.

Mennonites are now one of the great Christian world communions. They take their name from Menno Simmons, an early Anabaptist. They are very strong in the USA, but are found throughout the world. They are one of the historic peace churches.

Nominalism is from the disputes about universal ideas in the realm of philosophy and theology of the 14th Century, associated with William of Occam. Occam believed only individuals are real. Occam (or Ockham) was concerned with the status of knowledge.

Peace-church describes one of several groupings of Christian believers who take the teaching of the Sermon on the Mount with regard to peacemaking as one of the marks of the church. Such communities generally reject Christian ethical teaching on the just war and seek to develop strategies of non-violent change and conflict resolution. It is an activist response to a particular Gospel insight. The Society of Friends (Quakers) and the Mennonites are notable examples.

Radical Reformation describes the extreme edge of the Reformation of the 16th century. Throughout Europe the climate of change and reform engaged the hearts and minds of many people outside the formal structures of the Magisterial Reformers and governments. On the whole it refers to people who believed the Magisterial Reformers had stopped short of a true reformation.

Transubstantiation is a theological view developed in the 12th Century in the west to denote the conversion of the whole substance of the bread and wine in the Eucharist into the body and blood of Christ respectively. It is a doctrine which has been expressed in a variety of ways through the centuries in the light of changing emphases in philosophy and theology.

VIII   BIBLIOGRAPHY

Some older standard works are omitted from the list below because they are no longer generally available.

General Historical Background

Owen Chadwick, *The Reformation.* Pelican History of the Church, Penguin Books, 1964.

Norman Davies, *Europe: A History.* Oxford University Press, 1996; Paperback: Pimlico Press 1997.

Tim Dowley, *The History of Christianity.* Lion Publishing, 1977.

David L Edwards, *Christian England (revised edition).* Fount Paperbacks, 1989.

William R Estep, *Renaissance and Reformation.* William B Eerdmans, 1986.

Christopher Hill, *A Nation of Change and Novelty: Radical politics, religion and literature in seventeenth-century England.* Routledge, 1990.

Christopher Hill, *A Turbulent, Seditious and Factious People: John Bunyan and his Church.* Oxford University Press, 1988.

Christopher Hill, *The World Turned Upside Down: radical ideas during the English Revolution.* Penguin Books, 1975.

John McManners, ed. *The Oxford Illustrated History of the Christian Church.* Oxford University Press, 1990.

Christopher Rowland, *Radical Christianity.* Polity Press, 1988.

Gordon Rupp, *Patterns of Reformation.* Epworth Press, 1969.

Baptist History, Theology and Principles

Paul Beasley-Murray, *Radical Believers:The Baptist way of being the church.* Baptist Publications, 1992.

W H Brackney, *The Baptists.* Greenwood Press, 1988.

Richard Deats, *Ambassador of Reconciliation, A Muriel Lestor Reader.* New Society Publishers, 1991.

Paul R Dekar, *For the Healing of the Nations: Baptist Peacemakers.* Smyth & Helwys, 1993.

Ruth M B Gouldbourne, *Reinventing the Wheel: Women and Ministry in English Baptist Life.* Whitley Publications, 1997.

Roger Hayden, *English Baptist History and Heritage.* Baptist Publications, 1990.

Brian Haymes, *A Question of Identity.* Yorkshire Baptist Association, 1986.

H Leon McBeth, *The Baptist Heritage: Four centuries of Baptist Witness.* Broadman Press, 1987.

James William McClendon Jnr, *Systematic Theology : Volume 1 (Ethics)* and *Volume 2 (Doctrine).* Abingdon Press, 1986(1) and 1994(2).

Parker, Keith G *Baptists in Europe: History and Confessions of Faith.* Broadman Press, Tennessee, 1982.

Ian Sellers, *Edwardians, Anabaptists and the Problem of Baptist Origins, The Baptist Quarterly* Vol XXIX, Number 3, July 1981.

Walter B Shurden, *The Baptist Identity: Four Fragile Freedoms.* Smythe & Helwys, 1993.

Albert W Wardin, ed. *Baptists Around the World: A Comprehensive Handbook.* Broadman and Holman, 1995.

B R White, *The English Baptists of the 17th Century (revised).* Baptist Historical Society, 1996.

Nigel G Wright, *Power and Discipleship: Towards a Baptist Theology of the State.* Whitley Publications, 1996.

Anabaptist Studies

Torsten Bergsten, *Balthasar Hubmaier: Anabaptist Theologian and Martyr.* Judson Press, 1978

Thieleman J van Bracht, *Martyrs Mirror of Fifteen Centuries of Christian Martyrdom From the Time of Christ to AD1660.* Translated by Joseph F Sohm. Herald Press, Nineteenth English printing, 1997.

James Robert Coggins, *John Smyth's Congregation: English Separatism, Mennonite influence and the Elect Nation.* Herald Press, 1991.

Robert Friedmann, *The Theology of Anabaptism.* Herald Press, 1973.

Walter Klaassen, *Anabaptism Revisited.* Herald Press, 1992.

Marlene Kropf and Eddy Hall, *Praying with the Anabaptists: The Secret of Bearing Fruit.* Faith and Life Press, 1994.

John D Rempel, *The Lord's Supper in Anabaptism: A Study in the Christology of Balthasar Hubmaier, Pilgram Marpeck and Dirk Philips.* Herald Press, 1993.

C Arnold Snyder, *Anabaptist History and Theology: An Introduction.* Kitchener, Ontario, Pandora Press, 1997.

C Arnold Snyder, *The Life and Thought of Michael Sattler.* Herald Press, 1984.

Contemporary reflection on some of the issues

Tony Benn, *The Levellers and the English Democratic Tradition. Agenda for Prophets:Towards a Political Theology for Britain,* ed: Rex Ambler and David Haslam. Bowerdean Press, 1980.

Rodney Clapp, *A Peculiar People: the church as culture in a post-Christian society.* Inter-Varsity Press (USA), 1996.

Core Values. A report arising out of the Baptist Union Denominational Consultation in 1996, presented to the Baptist Union Council, March 1998. Baptist publications, 1998.

Walfred J Fahrer, *Building on the Rock: A Biblical Vision of Being Church Together from an Anabaptist-Mennonite Perspective.* Herald Press, 1995.

Keith G Jones, *What Value Democracy? Baptist Perspectives,* Bloomsbury, 1997.

Richard L Kidd, ed. *Something to Declare: A Study of the Declaration of Principle.* Whitley Publications, 1996.

Richard L Kidd, ed. *On the Way of Trust.* Whitley Publications, 1997.

Alan Kreider, *Journey Towards Holiness: A way of living for God's nation.* Marshall Pickering, 1986.

Eleanor Kreider, *Communion Shapes Character.* Herald Press, 1997.

Konrad Raiser, *To be the Church: Challenges and Hopes for a New Millennium.* WCC, 1997.

Haddon Willmer, ed. *Twenty:Twenty Vision: The Future of Christianity in Britain.* SPCK, 1992.

Nigel G Wright, *Challenge to Change.* Kingsway, 1991.

John Howard Yoder, *The Politics of Jesus.* Eerdmans, 1972.

Other Resources

Anabaptism Today. Magazine of the Anabaptist Network. Published three times per year. Details from 23 Barnes Close, Farnborough, Hants. GU14 7JA.
(See especially Issue 14, February 1997 and Issue 16, October 1997).

The Anabaptist Network can be contacted via Andrew Francis, 78 Marlborough Cresecent, Montreal Park, Sevenoaks, Kent TN13 2HR.

The Anabaptist Theological Study Circle. Co-Convenors Alan Kreider and Keith Jones.

London Mennonite Centre

Metanoia Book Service, 14 Shepherds Hill, London N6 5AQ